The Log Home Owner's Manual

A Guide to Restoring and Protecting Exterior Wood

By Jim Renfroe

Copyright 1995 Jim Renfroe

Distributed by *Wood Care Systems*
www.woodcaresystems.com

751 Kirkland Ave.
Kirkland, WA 98033
(800) 827-3480
(425) 827-6000
Fax (425) 822-5800

Dedication

I would like to dedicate this book to the two most important people in my life. My father, Lane Renfroe, who has been my mentor and coach throughout my business career and my wife, Lyla Renfroe, whose support and encouragement have kept me on task during the flurry of activity that surrounds our lives.

Acknowledgments

Thanks to the following people who have contributed their advice, information, encouragement and/or time to help me complete this book: Roland Sweet, Paula Bradley, Larry Cerenzie, Jeff Smith, John Mejlander, Bill Reckels, Bill Feist, Lonnie Williams, Brian Buchanon, Jean Steinbrecher, Lane Renfroe, and the dozens of customers that bought this book months ago and have patiently waited for its release.

Disclaimer

While the methods in this book have been successfully used over and over, wood is infinitely variable. Therefore, there is no one way that works the best, all of the time, on all wood species. This book gives the reader many tools to work with and several concepts about wood in general that should give the reader a broader understanding about the task at hand. Neither the author, publisher, editor or illustrator will be held liable for any incidental or consequential damages that may occur during this process. This information is believed to be true and accurate.

Table of Contents

Focus of the Book

his book focuses on **restoration** and **protection** of homes less than 30 years old. While many of the techniques and products used to refresh a five or ten year old home can also help to restore a 150 year old log home, these older log homes often have structural problems with the foundation, rotten logs, bad design, no electricity or running water and are not the kind of homes that make up the majority of today's log structures. Homes in the 5-30 year old range make up over 80% of the log homes that exist today. Many, if not most of them need some kind of maintenance today...right now. This can involve anything from a good rinse with a water hose and a new coat of finish, to some caulk in the joints, to treating areas of rot or insect infestation, to a full chemical strip down to bare wood and a full preservative system. Whatever the case may be, log home maintenance is not a one shot deal. Annual inspections and periodic maintenance are the keys to keeping the wood protected and looking good indefinitely.

This book is an owner's manual and should become a part of the log home. Just as the owner's manual in a car stays with the car when it's sold, this book should transfer to the new owners along with the title. There is a section in the back for notes and maintenance to record, along with inspection checklists and suggestions.

1

Introduction

Today's log home is a modern version of the housing that the early colonists lived in. It is an alternative to traditional housing that adds the warmth and beauty that only wood can offer. Log home building has existed for hundreds, if not thousands of years. The advent of tools that would cut and shape wood, became the advent of log homes. Before there  were sawmills, they were the only wood homes that could be put together with the resources of nature and the sweat of the early pioneers. After they settled into their surroundings, they began building another log home, better than the first, that they would move in to. The first structure usually became the barn. This gradual improvement continued for many years until the early industrialization of America began. Log homes were abandoned for modern homes, built on concrete foundations with framed walls covered with siding or stucco.

Somewhere around the 1960's there was a rebirth of interest in log homes. A few mills sprang up here and there, producing house logs that fit snugly together and met current building standards. Very slowly, this interest gave way to a full blown industry, and log homes began to be turned out in production facilities all over the country. Homes were being built and sold as fast as they could be produced, and an industry was born.

The log home industry continues to grow and prosper. Log home design and construction techniques have greatly improved since the boom times of the mid 80's when the market demand hit its first high peak. The biggest advances were in engineering and modern sealing systems. There were over 20,000 log homes per year being produced back then and many of them were sold as "maintenance free" homes. Therefore, many of them have not been maintained. This lack of maintenance manifests itself not only in unsightly log homes, black with mold and dark gray from weathering, but also rot, insect infestation, draftiness, and water infiltration. The purpose of this book is to teach the reader how to identify, correct and prevent problems with woods as Mother Nature takes her toll. These are preventable problems with proper maintenance, but what do you do about a log home that already has these problems?

Forward

In September of 1993 I gave a presentation on Log Home Maintenance at the International Log Builders Conference at Yellowstone National Park. There were log builders there from all over the world. I met log builders from New Zealand, Japan, Russia, Finland, England and Germany. It was held over a 4 day period with some advanced classes beginning before and some lasting after, but the main event was 4 days. The conference was subdivided into work groups, many of which were going on concurrently so one had to pick and choose which presentation he was going to attend. There were over 400 log builders there and I had no idea how many were going to show up for my part of the program. I did have a pretty good idea that it would not be one of the more popular events for a person that builds and sells new homes for a living. I was right. Log home maintenance is a much bigger concern for the log home owner, than the log home builder.

The 60 or so that came to my presentation included: Japanese and Korean delegations, industry publications, chinking and caulking suppliers, wood preservative suppliers, log inspectors and a few other peripheral industries. There were even a few log home builders, but not nearly as many as needed to be there. Log home maintenance for the most part is not a priority for most people in the business of selling new log homes. It is an issue that almost always come up in the selling process, but the prospective homeowner rarely gets a real idea of what he's in for. There has never been a concise, comprehensive answer to the issues of log home maintenance and after my presentation, several people asked for a copy of my notes and suggested I write a book. So here it is.

In this book, we're going to look at how to Clean, Preserve, Treat,

Seal and Maintain log homes. Often, bits and pieces of information about log home maintenance get contradicted from source to source and the homeowner ends up confused and frustrated. I hope to untangle some of the theories out there and get you on the right track. However, wood and weather are not always the same. What works on southern pine in Georgia, may not work on cedar in Oregon. Therefore, I'm going to try and explain the aging process of wood. Then, we'll look at some different ways to go about slowing it down, stopping it when possible and generally, how to postpone it for as long as possible. I wish I could figure out how to do this with people!

First we'll look at a brief explanation on the cellular makeup of wood as it relates to fluid movement into and out of logs. Then we'll look at some of the more common problems that we've all seen with not just house logs, but wood in general. Then we'll look at various wood cleaning methods, preservative systems, finishes and sealant systems. The last thing we'll cover is log home inspection, maintenance and proper protection of wood.

My basis for this book is a culmination of almost 20 years of wood preserving experience. My father owned a company that distributed chemicals for sapstain control in sawmills. It evolved into a manufacturer of pentachloraphenol and CCA that were used as wood preservatives in the pressure treating industry. I worked for my father all through high school and college, mixing chemicals and making deliveries. When I finished college, I began traveling with the salesmen all over the country visiting sawmills and wood preserving plants. As the business grew, I moved to North Carolina and built another production facility to help the company to keep up with the exploding demand for chemicals that would extend the life of wood many times over. After a few years, I moved to Vancouver, British Columbia to develop the market for our wood preservatives in Canada and the west coast of the United States. Meanwhile our family business was acquired by a large multinational company from the UK. My job was to bring some of the parent company's wood preserving technology in Europe to the US markets. These products were boron and copper based preservatives that were being used in Europe for treatment of railroad crossties, beams and utility poles after they had been in service several years. It was then that I began to realize how much wood was out there, in various stages of decay. Often there seemed nothing to do about it except replace it when it was too rotten to serve any useful purpose. The economics were overwhelming. For example a utility pole costs about $1500 to replace, but less than $100 to treat it in place every 5 years, which could extend it's life indefinitely.

One of my first new targets was the log home industry. Coming from the industrial wood preserving industry, I was appalled at the numbers of log homes that were being built with no treatment whatsoever. I began to hear horror stories about rotten and rotting house logs and could not understand why anyone would build a log home out of untreated wood. I have seen first hand, all of the problems that are discussed in this book. I have witnessed the results of neglected maintenance and have helped repair the damage. In 1988 I left the company that my father had started and began working toward the start of my own business. My career experience has been that of a supplier of wood preservatives, coatings and sealants in both industrial, as well as remedial markets. I have met several of the top wood scientists in the world in my travels to industry association meetings. I have sat through countless presentations on preservative systems, both old and experimental. I have had the opportunity to discuss log home maintenance with many of these acquaintances and have tried to translate those highly technical discussions into plain English. I hope that you learn from reading this book and find it both informative and understandable.

Part One

There seems to be a certain life-style associated with log homes. They exude tranquility and rustic elegance. They are often located away from the mainstream of life in the fast lane. When you enter a log home, there's a serene excitement that welcomes you. The warm environment of a log home induces comfort and relexation. Log home owners are usually proud home owners, they often open their home to total strangers who knock on the door and sheepishly ask to look inside, only dreaming of owning a log home themselves.

Building with logs offers excellent insulation from the elements and pound for pound has three times more strength than steel. It is relatively easy to work with, and lends itself to a multitude of architectural creations. Building homes with logs is an art form, and if properly protected and maintained will be a bequest for many generations to come.

Chapter One
Wood In General

Wood is made up of lignin and cellulose. Lignin binds the cells together and makes up about 15 to 30% of the dry wood's volume, depending on the species. Cellulose is the fibrous material that constitutes 70 to 85% of the dry wood. It is the cellulose that make up the cells. Wood cells are oblong, cigar shaped and have openings in both ends. They are arranged in such a way that water and nutrients pass in both directions through the cells. They are arranged end to end so that they can transport water and nutrients up from the roots all the way to the tip of each leaf. They also allow chemicals, produced through photosynthesis in the leaves, to be transported down to the roots. Water is critical to a live tree and makes up a large percentage of it's weight. <u>Trees are designed to move water</u> through tiny pips that run the full length of the tree. <u>Wood is an organic material and will decompose</u> rather quickly, given the right circumstances.

Wood Cells

 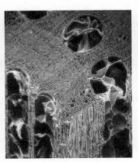 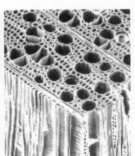

Nonporous Wood   *Ring-Porous Wood*   *Diffuse-Porous Wood*
Photo Courtesy of the Exterior Wood in the South Publication

11

The Life Cycle of Wood

When a tree is alive, it has natural defense mechanisms that ward off disease and enemies like termites, beetles and decay. Sometimes a disease can overwhelm this natural immune system and cause a living tree to die, but more often live trees are cut down on purpose.

When a tree is cut down, it's defense mechanisms are cut off and there are a host of natural processes that begin to take place almost immediately. Blue stain or log stain, for example can begin within 24 hours if the conditions are right. The first thing that usually happens is an invasion of microorganisms that feed on the wood sugars in the surface of the log, just under the bark. This process makes the surface more porous, which causes the log to retain more water, making it a comfortable home for decay fungi. Decay fungi weaken the cell walls and cause a loss in both strength and mass. Meanwhile, beetles can infest the bark and begin to use the wood as a food source. Termites can also set up shop. Over a period of a decade or so, the once magnificent tree is reclaimed by Mother Nature.

This oversimplified explanation applies to any species of wood, in any area of the world, although the period of time in which it happens will be vastly different. The good news is that you can interrupt this natural process and postpone it indefinitely. The key is that you have to stay one step ahead of Mother Nature. She's taking a proactive role in the process, so you also have to be proactive. There are things regarding your home that you may need to react to right now. There may be damage already done, but <u>Don' Worry</u>! That's why you bought this book. In most cases you can stop it and postpone it's reoccurrence for a long, long time.

Water In Wood

When a tree is alive, water makes up a large portion of it's weight and volume. When the tree is cut down it begins to lose this water and shrinks mostly in diameter, and to a much lesser degree, in length. Logs will shrink in diameter about 4-6% on the average. As the log gradually gets smaller in diameter, tremendous stresses can build up on the log surface, and since wood doesn't stretch or compress, tiny fissures form, then enlarge to become cracks or checks in the log. This process can continue for 2 to 3 years, and is usually over by the 5th year. Checks are a potential source of air and water infiltration into the home as well as a reservoir for rainwater to collect. This could lead to rot. There is a section later on in the book that deals with checks. Some log builders make a cut or kerf along the length of the log, usually on the underside as an artificial check. When done to the proper depth, this actually helps control checking on the more visible surfaces of the logs.

Most of the liquid water is lost through the ends of the logs or boards since it is easily transported along the pipelines that exist in the wood. Water vapor also passes along this pipeline, but also passes out of the logs radially, and through the checks. This is why you should use a breathable finish on the logs, so water vapor can pass through the finish. Otherwise, it could get trapped behind a non-breathing film and cause moisture damage, mold growth or in some cases, it can push the film off the wood, creating flaking and peeling.

A non-breathable film may crack and peel in less than two years.
Photo Courtesy of the Exterior Wood In the South Publication

13

Chapter Two
Typical Problems With Wood

The two biggest problems in wood come from either moisture or ultraviolet radiation. **Moisture** is the key element of anything that can destroy the structural integrity of your log home. Dry wood won't attract destructive insects. Dry wood won't rot. Dry wood won't grow mildew colonies. Dry wood won't discolor from metal fasteners. Moisture is natural in wood and so is everything that turns wood into compost. <u>Keep your wood dry and you rule out a multitude of problems.</u>

The second biggest problems with wood are caused by **Ultraviolet Radiation** from the sun. UV rays destroy the lignin portion of the wood, leaving loose wood fibers subject to erosion and abrasion. Sunlight is also the biggest enemy of wood finishes, so they must be reapplied at least every 3-5 years if you use a good one, and every year if you use a cheap one.

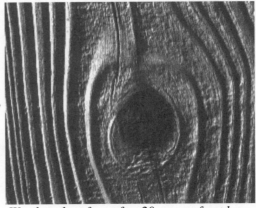

Weathered surface after 20 years of outdoor exposure.

Photo Courtesy of the
Exterior Wood in the South Publication

Using a pigmented wood finish with mildewcides and fungicides is a must. I know of no penetrating clear wood finish that offers UV protection, however, there are several that make the claim. There are very complex situations that happen to wood when bombarded with UV Radiation. I firmly believe that someday there will be unpigmented finishes that provide long term UV protection, but it's still a ways off.

Before the use of proper designs and wood preservatives, log homes were abandoned when they reached various stages of deterioration.

Chapter Three

Mold and Mildew

Mold and mildew are commonly used interchangeably in the log home industry. As a matter of fact, I know one guy who calls it MOLDEW. Mold is more common on house logs, but mildew also occurs. They are both caused by microscopic airborne spores landing on nutrient rich wood surfaces, germinating and then multiplying into colonies. They are also both killed by bleach or other chlorinated products. Mold is a term often applied to black, blue, green, and red fungal growths. Mildew refers to whitish growths, however there are differences. The bottom line is, they are caused by the same set of circumstances, prevented by the same methods and killed by the same treatments. If that's all you want to know about "moldew" then skip to the next section. Otherwise, read on for an explanation of what these guys are all about.

Mold

Mold is a fuzzy, cobweb like growth, produced on organic matter by several types of fungi. Black mold *(Aspergillus niger)*, one of the most familiar molds, begins as a microscopic, airborne spore that germinates on contact with the moist surface of nonliving organic matter, like wood. It spreads rapidly, forming the mycelium (fungal body), which is made up of a fine network of filaments (hyphae). The mycelium produces other clusters of root like hyphae called rhizoids, which penetrate the wood surface, secreting enzymes, then absorbing water and the digested sugars and starches. Other clusters of hyphae then reach upward, which bear the particular color of the mold species. Upon ripening, they break open and the airborne spores land elsewhere and begin to reproduce.

Molds thrive on a great many organic substances and provided with sufficient moisture, they rapidly disintegrate wood, paper and leather. Besides being destructive however, molds also have many industrial uses, such as in the fermentation of organic acids and cheeses. Camembert and Roquefort cheeses for example, gain their particular flavors from the enzymes of *Penicillium camemberti* and *Penicillium roquesforti*, respectively. Penicillium, a product of the green mold *Penicillium notatum*, revolutionized antibiotic drugs after its discovery in 1929, and the red bread mold *Neurospora* is an important tool in genetic experiments.

Moldy wood is usually a precursor to rot or decay. Severe cases in concentrated areas, like around the corners or base logs, indicate a moisture problem that may be addressed with gutters, flashing or other drainage solutions. Mold grows anytime the temperature is above freezing, but when it is above about 70° F or 20°C, it will thrive. Mold needs three things to survive:
    1) a warm temperature
    2) a food source
    3) moisture
Take away any one of the three and mold will not grow. When logs have been freshly peeled or milled, the sap comes to the surface and ends. This makes a nutritious and hearty meal for an up and coming mold spore. Mold spores are like tiny airborne seeds that are present in almost every region of the world. If they land on a surface that has the right combination of temperature, food and humidity, they will grow and multiply into large colonies.

Tree sap and wood in general, is full of wood sugars and other nutrients that mold organisms like to eat. If the climatic conditions can support mold, green logs should be coated with an appropriate preservative at the log yard as quickly as possible after they have been peeled. Preferably within 24 hours to prevent mold from starting. These treatments basically poison the wood as a food supply, killing any existing colonies and preventing others from starting. However, if mold has already started and you kill it, there could still be some discoloration which can be cleaned with bleach, oxalic acid or by other methods that will be discussed later.

Mildew

Mildew is the term popularly applied to visible growth of fungi or bacteria on wet clothes, food or other objects. Scientifically, the term is restricted to members of either of two families of fungus that are parasitic on living plants and to the plant diseases they produce. The two families are *Peronosporaceae*, comprising the down mildews and *Eryisphaceae*, comprising the powdery mildews. The powdery mildews are parasitic chiefly on the leaves of plants and are so called because of their numerous white spores that produce a powdery, cobwebbed pattern on the leaves. Attacks of powdery mildew cause curling

Mildew on naturally weathered siding.
Photo Courtesy of the Exterior Wood in the South Publication

and withering of leaves and often prevent new shoots on the plant. Powdery mildew usually attacks plants grown in the shade in humid regions.

Sapstain/Blue Stain

Blue Stain grows on the surface of the wood and works its way toward the heartwood. It produces irreversible discoloration, but it does not destroy the wood. Like other molds, it does increase the wood's porosity so it absorbs water more rapidly and takes longer to dry out. Blue stain can usually be identified by its color and is very evident at the log ends, were it can appear as streaks starting at the outside of the log, tapering toward the heart of the log. Clever lumber brokers began marketing "blue stained pine"

several years ago like it was a special process that they developed to decorate wood. I continue to see it used for doors and interior paneling. Once the wood is dry, the staining organisms die and further "bluing" does not occur.

Blue stain

Photo Courtesy of the United States Forest Service

Fungi

Fungi is a diverse group of either single-celled or multicellular organisms that obtain food by direct absorption of nutrients. The food is dissolved by enzymes that the fungi excrete and is then absorbed by the fungal organism. <u>Together with bacteria, fungi are responsible for the decay and decomposition of all organic matter and are found wherever other forms of life exist.</u> Approximately 100,000 species of fungi are known.

Structure

Most fungi are composed of delicate tubes known as hyphae. Hyphae grow by elongation at the tips and also by branching. Abundant development of hyphae may result in the formation of large fruiting structures such as mushrooms and puffballs. If you see these on your house logs and the decay is very advanced, replace those particular logs, then closely inspect the surrounding ones.

Reproduction

Most fungi reproduce by spores, which are tiny airborne seeds. The common mushroom may form 12 billion or more spores on it's fruiting body; the giant puffball may produce several trillion.

Fungi Physiology

Fungi require free oxygen and large amounts of water and carbohydrates for growth. Sugars such as glucose and levulose, common factors in wood, are usable by most fungus. Some fungi may use nitrogen from the atmosphere. Oxalic acid and other organic acids such as citric, formic, pyruvic, succinic, malic and acetic acids are formed by many fungi.

Fungi Ecology

Spores are carried for long distances in the atmosphere. Water habitats are often abundant with water molds. A number of spores are also frequent in either fresh or salt water. In recent years many fungi have been discovered in polluted rivers and streams. These fungi participate in the natural decomposition of sewage. Some of these species are of special interest because they cause diseases in humans.

Certain fungi live in a symbiotic association with algae, forming characteristic structures known as lichens. These lichens are more common in the Pacific Northwest regions and grow in abundance on cedar roofing materials.

Some fungi, which ordinarily grow on dead organic matter, are capable of infecting live plants when given the opportunity. Others cannot exist except as parasites of living plants. Diseases caused by fungus include: clubroot of cabbage, powdery scab of potatoes, potato wart, white rusts, potato late blight, spot anthracnoses, chestnut blight, Dutch elm disease, oak wilt, ergot, brown rot of stone fruits and numerous others.

Many small animals, insects and millipedes eat fungi and thus are instrumental in spore distribution. Some groups of insects cultivate fungi as food. Ambrosia beetles and certain groups of termites are particularly important to the log home.

The Good Side of Fungi
The enzymes of fungi are useful for a number of industrial processes. When grown on steamed wheat bran or rice bran, one fungal species produces an amylase product useful in alcoholic fermentation. Proteases obtained from another fungus are used in the manufacturing of liquid glue. Commercial production of industrial ethyl alcohol is accomplished by fermentation of sugarcane molasses or hydrolyzed starch by means of enzymes formed by another fungus. In the process of making bread, yeast is added to dough to produce carbon dioxide. Fungi is also used for the commercial production of citric acid, and in the production of gluconic acid and gallic acid, which is used in the manufacture of inks and dyes. Synthetic resins are manufactured from fumaric acid formed by black bread mold. Gibberellic acid, which promotes increased growth of plant cells, is formed by a fungus causing disease in rice plants. Commercially usable oils have been obtained from species of several genera, and one species is a practical source of edible proteins. Vitamin D is prepared by irradiation of ergosterol, a substance which may be obtained from the waste brewer's yeast. A yeast-like fungus is a source of riboflavin, and biotin accumulates during production of fumaric acid by another fungus. Fungi are also used to produce Roquefort cheese and to ripen Camembert cheese.

22

Fungi have been used medicinally since ancient times. Ergot alkaloids are also a source of lysergic acid diethylamide, commonly known as LSD, which produces hallucinogenic effects, often of a severe nature. The use of antibiotics in medical practice dates from recognition of the antibiotic properties of penicillin.

Common types of decay fungi to log homes are:

• *White Rot*

White rot usually occurs in the sapwood only. Wood with white rot will usually shrink and collapse when severely degraded. White rotted wood appears lighter or white and somewhat stringy.

• *Brown Rot*

Brown rot cracks across the grain and then shrinks away from the rest and collapses.

• *Dry Rot*

Dry rot is the same as brown rot. It looks dry because it's all cracked up, <u>but dry wood won't rot.</u> Rot won't grow unless the moisture content is above 20%. "Dry" rot is really a misnomer.

• *Soft Rot*

Soft rot does not cause near the structural damage as any of it's cousins. It is generally pretty shallow, but is very unsightly. It is not a real threat to log homes, but is common in fences and wood roofing.

• *Bracket Fungi*

Bracket fungi are fruiting bodies that protrude from the wood's surface and are bad news for the affected logs. They are akin to mushrooms. They normally grow on wood that is already rotten. If you see bracket fungi, those logs will probably need to be replaced.

Chapter Four
Wood Destroying Insects

Other enemies to house logs include several types of insects. Some of these pesky insects may actually digest the wood, while others may only tunnel through the logs to build nests.

Carpenter Ants

Carpenter ants do not digest wood. They tunnel through it to feed on other insects and to build nests. The good news is, the nests in the house are seldom large enough to cause structural damage. The bad news is, the nests they build in a house are rarely the main nest. The main nest is usually out away from the house in a wood pile or tree stump. You have to kill the main nest to kill the colony. There are many methods and chemicals that work on carpenter ants. The pest exterminators usually use a combination of treatments, including barrier treatments under the drip line or eaves and perimeter treatments around

Carpenter Ant

the yard. They will use products like liquid diazanon, tempo or dursban. Make sure they treat the area around any dead trees, limbs, stumps or firewood piles. There has been limited success with borates in treating active infestations, but if your house logs are already borate treated, the carpenter ant will probably decide that your neighbor's house would be a better place to set up shop. If you can find the nest in the house, chemicals can be injected directly into the nest. If you can find the main nest and kill the queen, your ant problems will soon be over. Carpenter ants usually make the migration from the satellite nest to the main nest at night, about 5 or 6 hours after dark. I've heard of people walking their yards at midnight with a flashlight looking for the parade of carpenter ants and then following it to the main nest. For the diehard "do-it-yourselfer", this may be OK. However, it may be easier to do barrier and perimeter treatments and hope for the best. It's kind of like building a poisonous moat around your home and yard. They supposedly make that migration every night. If they don't wipe their feet, and bring poison into their nest, they will infect the nest. Carpenter ants are cannibalistic, so if one dies from an overdose of dursban, the others will eat him and they too will die. When they die they get eaten and soon the colony is wiped out from a lack of balanced diet. The alternative course is to find the main nest and gas it all at once with ant poison.

It usually takes anywhere from a few weeks to a few months to control a carpenter ant problem, so don't expect immediate results. Don't hesitate to get the exterminator back out there if their mission is not accomplished.

By the way, **never** stack firewood against the house or on your wood deck. You're inviting problems from decay, insects and mold.

Termites

Termites are a problem in temperate climates from coastal British Columbia to Mexico and from California to Florida, then north to New York. Termites live in groups as a society and can be very

Termite

26

severe in their destruction. If you have termites, borate treatments can be very effective. However, monitor and retreat until the problem is over and don't hesitate to call an exterminator. If the problem is severe, the exterminator may suggest tenting the house and fumigating it with nasty poisonous gas that may or may not penetrate large diameter logs. This is a very expensive proposition and you should definitely get a second opinion. Also, discuss the problem with your county extension agent. He or she will usually know all of the bugs in your area by name, and can offer an unbiased opinion on what to do.

Beetles

There are more beetles than any other insect. There are over 30,000 species of beetles and they make up about 40% of the entire insect population. However, there are only three families of beetles that commonly feed on seasoned wood. All beetles have chewing type mouth parts, in both the larval and adult stages The most common characteristic found in beetles in the adult stage, is the presence of four wings. The front pair is hard and leathery, while the back pair is very thin, like a membrane.

Beetles undergo a complete metamorphosis during their development. The damage they do to wood is done primarily in the larval stage, when they look more like a worm than a beetle. The larval stage of a wood boring beetle is always spent inside the wood. As the larvae eat the wood, they grow and develop into adults. As adults, they bore their way out of the wood and escape. Sometimes they exit the log and end up on the inside of the home. This is when panic sets in, but there is little that can be done about it. They should not pose a further problem to your wood, but if they're crawling around the inside of your home, spray them with an insecticide designed for crawling insects when you see them. The adult beetle should not be considered a threat to your seasoned wood. He's had his fill of that and the only thing on his mind is finding a cute little female to mate with. However, if you see one, you can bet your bottom dollar that he just emerged from one of your logs. He's probably been there for many months or perhaps years, and has no intention of returning. He's been there all his life and like most adolescents, he ate a lot and left a trail of destruction. If the beetle is lucky enough not to be eaten by a bird, or sprayed with Black Flag, it will live outside until it digs itself into a live tree and lays eggs. Then it dies and so goes the life of a beetle.

As mentioned earlier, there are only a few types of beetles that eat wood. Below is a description of each one:

• *Powder Post Beetles*

Powder post beetles are more of a problem since they actually eat wood as a food source and can cause deterioration in some logs. Usually, they do not dig real deep. The holes they leave are small, about 1/8 inch and are more oval than round. They can be controlled with borate based preservatives if the moisture in the wood is high enough to allow the borates to diffuse into where the bugs are. Again, an exterminator can be your best source for solutions to these six-legged, four-winged problems.

Powder Post Beetle

• *Old House Borers*

Old house borers are more common in the mid-Atlantic states and can also be very destructive. They rank second to termites in their destruction to wood. As the name implies, they infest well-seasoned wood. However, they will also attack unseasoned wood if the conditions are right. They do not normally attack hardwoods, only coniferous softwoods.

Old House Borer

28

The adult beetle is about 1/2 to 1 inch long. If you look at it with a magnifying glass you will notice that it has gray hairs on it's head. The larva can be up to about 1 1/4 inch long. There are three eyespots on each side of it's head which distinguish this guy from other beetle larva. They are also very loud munchers. I've heard of people being kept awake at night from old house borers munching and gnawing their way through the wood. Call an exterminator if you suspect old house borers and make sure the noise you hear is not your bed mate grinding his or her teeth.

The good news is that bug research indicates that in a heated, well ventilated, occupied log home, re-infestation beyond one generation is rare. In other words, if you have old house borers now, their offspring will probably leave your logs and not come back. Therefore, don't spend a zillion bucks having your house tented and fumigated, because chances are your problem will be short lived.

Non-Chemical Insect Control

One of the main factors that is common with most beetle infestations, is moisture in the wood. It is a well documented fact that no wood boring beetle will develop rapidly in wood that is very dry. Indications point to the fact that most beetles cannot exist in wood with a moisture content below about 15%. Old house borers can get by in wood as low as about 10%, but their level of activity is greatly reduced.

The challenge then, is to get the wood as dry as possible and keep it that way. Vapor barriers under the house and in the roof system will make a dramatic difference. Central heating systems can dry the wood out and keep it dry. Water repellent finishes that are maintained so they keep logs from getting wet are critical. Every effort you can think of should be employed to keep your logs dry. This will create an undesirable environment for wood destroying organisms and prevent a host of problems, including insect attack, decay and discoloration.

29

Carpenter Bees

Carpenter bees do not destroy wood. They do some tunneling and can usually be controlled with insecticide additives you mix in with your exterior finish. They are available through most paint stores (but don't let them sell you stain unless they can give you a couple of customers that have had that stain on their homes for more than 2 years). When they walk across it, the bees die. Pest control companies have access to a much wider array of chemicals than you can get over the counter, so don't hesitate to contact your local Orkin man for carpenter bees, or any other insects that you have, or suspect you have.

Carpenter Bee

Chapter Five
Ultraviolet Light

Weathering problems are the most common aesthetic problems that the log home owner faces. Of all of the weather problems there are, **Ultraviolet Light**, causes the most destruction of wood surfaces and finishes. In scientific terms this is known as *photooxidation*. It happens at the molecular level and is actually a chemical process brought on by absorption of the solar energy which kicks off the reaction. The adverse consequences of UV light irradiation are discoloration, chemical modification of the wood cells, and deterioration of the cell walls. Therefore, the changes brought about by *photooxidation*, open the doors to further damage to wood cells. The good news is that it happens on the surface of the logs and causes no structural problems. The bad news is that the surface of the log is what you see, and the problem is, that it's ugly.

It only takes about two months before signs of UV damage become very noticeable. Research at the Forest Products Lab in Wisconsin, suggests that unprotected wood begins to show signs of damage within 2 weeks. As this damage progresses, the wood's surface becomes less able to hold a finish, and therefore should be coated with a protective finish as soon as possible.

The first coat of a wood finish should be designed to penetrate the wood's surface and prepare the surface for a second coat. However, be aware that the transparent finishes used on most log homes, need to be maintained every few years. Never let the home go more than five years without a good cleaning and a maintenance coat of finish that provides protection from UV, water and organic growth.

The sun also has an intense drying effect on wood, especially horizontal wood like decks, rails, steps and cedar roofs. Natural oils in wood become oxidized by the sun and washed out by the rain. Water based wood finishes do little to alter these natural processes. Usually however, <u>penetrating oils</u> do a much better job of protecting new wood or restoring weathered wood.

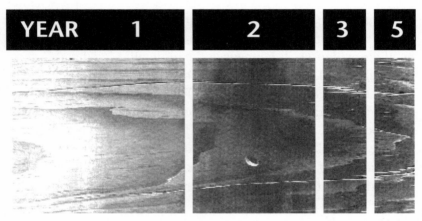

Artist's rendering of surface wood changes for a typical softwood during the outdoor weathering process.
Illustration Courtesy of the Exterior Wood in the South Publication

Chapter Six
Water Damage

Water acts as a secondary natural hazard to wood. Mold, mildew and fungi tend to thrive in damp conditions. Since these organisms cause the wood to become more porous, it absorbs more water and then takes longer to dry out, thus speeding the destructive process.

Water is truly a partner in crime with UV light. Once the UV radiation begins to break down the outer wood cells and fibers, rain will actually wash them away through erosion. This will expose fresh wood and the process will start all over again.

Someone made the observation that erosion of house logs is so slow that it would take 100 years to wash away a quarter inch of wood. I would not consider erosion in and of itself, a real threat to a log home.

The dark spots on the logs show mold and mildew growing as a result of unprotected logs.

However, unless your house logs were pressure treated or borate treated, most of the protection that you apply to a log home resides in the outer sixteenth of an inch. It is critically important to do everything you can to protect the wood's surface.

Proper protection of your wood with a finish that provides protection from water, mildew and UV light **is a must**. It will alleviate a host of problems that can occur with house logs. Please be sure to read the section on wood finishes later on in this book. It will explain how to select a good wood finish. Remember one thing. The worst thing you can do--is nothing at all.

Moss, mold and lichens on a wood roof. Don't forget, if you have a wood roof, the roof needs periodic care and maintenance too.

Chapter Seven
Design Criteria

The design of your log home can play a very important role in the upkeep of your home. A poor design will contribute to the damage caused by water.

• *Roof Overhangs*

The eaves of a roof should extend at least 2 feet beyond the log walls on a single story house and 4 feet for a two story house. This not only gets the rain water well away from the logs, but provides some shade from the sun. However, be aware that the bottom logs will not be shaded from the sun as much as the upper logs, and may require more frequent maintenance. Also, make sure that roof purlins do not extend beyond the roof overhangs. If they do, water will wick into the logs and they will weather and rot within a few years.

• *Foundation*

The foundation should be above grade and the sill logs should never be in contact with the ground unless they are pressure treated with CCA to a chemical retention of .4 pounds per cubic foot and inspected by a third party testing agency.

• *Ground Slope*

The grade should slope away from the home so that rainwater drains well away from the house and does not collect around the walls.

• *Gutters*

Gutters are a good way to route the water well away from the house. Also, without gutters, rain will fall from the roof and splash the bottom logs, getting them wet every time it rains. I once saw a log home where water from the second story roof fell onto the roof of the front porch. Water splashed back on the logs, just above where the porch roof joined the second story. The logs were so rotten that you could reach into the logs and grab hand-fuls of rotten wood. Gutters would have diverted the water through a downspout, away from the logs, preventing this catas-trophe from happening. The more you can do to keep water away from your logs, the less chance you will have of rot, mold and other wood damage.

• *Landscaping*

Keep shrubs and trees from touching the logs or roof. Trim plants back far enough to allow for air circulation and sunlight to reach the logs.

Water damage caused by lack of maintenance and poor designs have almost destroyed this wood structure. Carpet keeping the porch wet, as well as poor overhangs and gutters have contributed to the destruction.

36

Part Two

How to Clean, Preserve, Protect, Seal and Maintain an Existing Log Home

Proper care and maintenance of the wood in a log home can create a beautiful habitat and prevent a host of problems in the future. Maintaining a log home can more than double it's life expectancy. I believe that proper wood care and periodic maintenance will extend the useful life of wood indefinitely. But let's be realistic here. I hate to be the one to break the news to you, but house logs are really just **tree cadavers**. Once a tree is cut down, it no longer has defense mechanisms, like it did as a live tree. It is nature's way of recycling to send in scavengers like termites and decay fungi to return that tree to the earth. You have to take a proactive approach to interrupt these natural processes and postpone them. It can be done, and your log home can last and look good for many years, decades or even centuries. <u>The worst thing you can do is nothing at all.</u> The best thing you can do is to put your home on a maintenance program. The tables in

Log home maintenance is like maintaining a car, a lawn or even the human body. Preventative and ongoing maintenance can make for a lifetime of trouble free use. Lack of proper maintenance is an invitation for problems.

There are two basic steps in protecting wood: <u>surface preparation</u> and <u>application</u>. You must first start with clean wood. Whether the home is new or old, proper surface preparation is critical to a good finishing job.

Think of surface preparation on wood the same way you look at site preparation for construction of a log home on your lot. Without proper slope and drainage, no amount of digging will overcome the problems that could have been easily dealt with before the foundation was poured. Without attention to the orientation of the house on the lot, you may not have the view you wanted. Surface preparation is the same way. If you stain over dirty, moldy, rotten wood with a transparent finish, you will always see dirty, moldy, rotten wood underneath the finish. In fact, you could make it worse.

Proper application of preservatives, stains and finishes is equally important. Always read label instructions before you start the job. Call your supplier and clarify any questions you have before you start. While application varies from product to product, there are some general guidelines for you to follow. What follows is an overview of the basic steps to finishing wood.

Chapter Eight
Surface Preparation

As discussed, the first step to renewing your log home is cleaning the surface. This process may involve wood cleaners, strippers and mechanical finish removal.

There are several ways to clean dirty, weathered wood. Pressure washing is probably the most universal way, but may not always be possible, especially when there are openings between logs big enough to see daylight through. This could result in wet carpet or ruined artwork and furniture inside the home. If there are openings in the logs, seal them with caulk or chinking first, then power wash. However, it is best to spray a wood cleaner on the logs first. Here are some of the common types of surface cleaners.

• *Chlorinated Systems*

In certain forms, chlorine is a very strong cleaner, sanitizer and sterilizer. Household bleach is the most accessible and effective way to "sterilize" a wood surface. It will kill most, if not all, of the microorganisms that are present on your logs, allowing you to start with a clean slate. Household bleach is about 5-6% chlorine in the form of sodium hypochlorite. This may not sound like much, but believe me, it's plenty. Most of the time it works best when diluted to about 3%, so mix it with equal volumes of warm water. It remains active for about 45 minutes, so use it quickly.

The best way to use it is to wet the wood first with water. Don't saturate it, but wet the surface. Then apply the bleach and water solution and let it remain on the wood for about 10 minutes. Light scrubbing may be necessary on some areas. Then rinse it thoroughly until there is no longer a bleach smell or feel on the wood. If there are still mold stains visible, sand those areas with 80 grit sandpaper, then re-bleach and rinse.

How does chlorine work? In household bleach, the sodium hypochlorite combines with water to form hypochlorous acid. Hypochlorous acid is very unstable and will react with almost anything, including proteins and nitrogen compounds that comprise a mildew organism. The mildew basically dissolves and then can be rinsed away.

A word of warning about chlorine. Never mix ammonia or other cleaners that contain ammonia or acid, with chlorine. They can combine to form a deadly gas. However, if your wood is especially moldy or dirty, add 1/2 cup of TSP (Tri Sodium Phosphate) to a gallon of bleach and water. It will make an even stronger cleaner. You can also use this brew to clean decks, outdoor furniture and concrete.

The other thing to keep in mind with all wood cleaners, is that while most of them are pretty good at removing most of the mildew, dirt and discoloration that's on the surface, nothing is better than sandpaper for complete removal of surface stains.

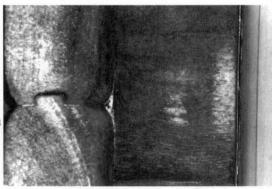

You can see that there is good wood underneath all of the grunge.

Look at it this way: If you get 90% of the surface clean with

42

wood cleaner, then you've just reduced your sanding job by 90%. A random orbital sander with 80 grit sandpaper, will take care of most of the surface problems with the least amount of effort. Just make sure the logs are free from all sanding dust before you apply the finish.

Be sure to rinse it thoroughly. Notice how long it takes to wash bleach off your hands. If you can smell bleach on your hands, there is still some there. Get the picture? Make sure you get it all off of your wood or it could interfere with the stains. Also, when applying bleach to moldy surfaces, <u>start from the bottom and work your way up.</u> Otherwise, you will have streaks that no amount of elbow grease will remove. Additionally, bleach and water have a tendency to cause the wood to develop a fuzzy appearance This is because bleach is a strong chemical and actually destroys some of the lignin in the wood. Loose wood fibers on the surface are the fuzz that appears. You can sand them off, or just stain over them. However, make sure at least the first coat of stain penetrates instead of building a film. A film must have a solid surface to bond to. Fuzzy wood due to loose wood fibers is not conducive to proper adhesion of films.

Swimming pool chlorine is a much stronger form of household bleach. It is calcium hypochlorite and can be purchased anywhere that pool chemicals are sold. Mix 2 or 3 ounces to a gallon of water. Let it dissolve for about 30 minutes before you use it. Not all of the crystals will dissolve, so mix it in a bucket first, then gently pour the solution into your sprayer, leaving the undissolved solids in the bucket. Unlike household bleach, it will remain active for several hours, allowing for a little more leeway.

Some researchers say that both forms of bleach causes wood fibers to become less porous, thus inhibiting penetration of stains and finishes. I think a lot depends on how long you leave it on the wood and how well it's rinsed. Therefore, since it only takes a few minutes to do the trick, don't take a lunch break until you've finished rinsing the bleach off your walls. You will minimize the problems that bleach may cause and capitalize on it's benefits.

Left:
Gray, weathered logs due to lack of water repellancy and UV protection..

Right:
Same logs after they were cleaned with an oxalic acid cleaner to remove dirt and UV weather, then pressure washed.

Prepared wood cleaners that contain bleach are much safer and gentler on the wood, as well as more user friendly. They usually contain surfactants to enable it to penetrate the surface better, buffers to lessen it's harshness to the wood fibers and thickeners to keep it from being as runny, causing major streaks as it runs down the wall. Most prepared bleach solutions are concentrates and are more expensive. However, you will probably end up with a better looking home and the process will be much easier. Follow the label directions. The makers of these products, usually know what they're talking about and have written the instructions based on trial and error. Do what they say, and above all else, relax and enjoy the magic of transforming your wood! And don't forget to rinse.

One last reminder before we leave the topic of chlorine. NEVER mix any chlorine containing product with an ammonia containing product. They react to form a DEADLY gas, which could cause to black out or even kill you. One time, in an effort to make a super-duper bathroom cleaner for the shower stall, my wife mixed up a little of this and that cleaner. She became very ill. Fortunately, she got out of there quick enough to avoid catastrophe, but she could have died from cleaning the shower.

• *Percarbonate Based Products*

Sodium peroxydicarbonate is a brightener. It is used in many wood cleaners that can be purchased at most building supply stores. Look at the list of ingredients or precautionary statements to find it. It is very safe, and is a very aggressive cleaner. It loosens dirt, grime and surface mold, so they can be gently scrubbed off or removed with a pressure washer. Let it work on the wood for about 15 minutes before you start scrubbing. Remember that if you scrub too much, you'll get fuzzy wood. Let the chemical do the hard part and use a very soft bristle brush to work the foam. Bristles too stiff can cause fuzzy wood. Rinse it thoroughly, then once again for good luck.

• *Oxalic Acid*

Oxalic acid is good for returning dirty and weathered gray wood to it's original color. It is also good at getting water stains out of wood, like where the sprinkler has been hitting the same spot for years. It can be used over some previously stained or painted surfaces. Wet down the wood first, apply the solution, let it work for 10 minutes, scrub it gently and rinse it thoroughly afterwards. Allow at least a couple of dry, sunny days before you stain.

The wood shows iron stains from a metal roof installation. Metal shavings got encapsolated under the finish and then started to oxidize.

<u>Oxalic acid is very good for removing iron stains or nail stains.</u> However, if there is a film of finish or preservative over it, you may have to remove the finish in order to get down to bare wood. Oxalic acid is very good to apply to weathered cedar and red-wood decks that have darkened due to tannin stains that are inherent in those wood species. Oxalic acid is the main ingredient in several cleaners available at paint stores and building material outlets. Look for it in the list of active ingredients and follow the label instructions.

You can buy it in bulk from your friendly neighborhood chemical distributor. In bulk means, 50 or 100 pounds at a time. Use a solution made up of about 2 cups of crystals per gallon of water or 1/2 to 1 pound per gallon (hot water dissolves the crystals faster). However, straight oxalic acid solutions can be very aggressive on wood surfaces and the <u>fumes can gag you</u>, so use extreme care. It is best to stay with prepared liquid solutions that contain buffers and surfactants, with oxalic acid as the main ingredient.

Oxalic acid is a natural derivative of the rhubarb plant. It comes from the leaves, which are poison. This is why you eat the stalks and not the leaves. When dealing with any of these chemicals, <u>use eye and skin protection and avoid getting it on plants.</u> As a precaution, wet down grass, plants the surrounding area

A deck shown before and after stripping..

before application, and rinse them down good afterwards. Wash your hands thoroughly before eating, smoking or using the bathroom. Chemical irritations are no fun, especially on tender areas.

• _Home Brew_

You can make an effective cleaner yourself, with Cascade dish washing soap. It contains some very effective surfactants and is less likely to cause the fuzzy wood phenomenon by itself. It cleans well and rinses easier than most cleaners. However, it's a good idea to wet the wood down first to keep the cleaning solution from soaking in so deep that it's hard to rinse. Mix about 1/2 cup of Cascade dish washing soap and a quart of bleach with 3 quarts of warm or hot water. Spray or brush it onto the logs, scrub as little as possible and rinse thoroughly. If the logs are still dirty, do it again and scrub a little harder. The object is to let the "soap" do most of the work without scrubbing the lignin off the wood, causing the hairlike appearance. Do a test area first to determine how long it should stay on the wood, how much pressure you need to apply to the brush as you scrub and how long it will take to rinse.

• _Potassium Salts of Fatty Acids_

Some of the organisms above are not affected by these chemicals. Some forms of moss, algae or lichen are best killed with potassium salts of fatty acids. These are very low toxicity chemicals and are marketed under the category of moss killers, etc. They must be applied when the moss is active, like when it's wet but not raining. The organism absorbs the chemical into itself and dies. This process could take a couple of weeks, but when they're dead, they can easily be removed with a broom, brush or by light power washing.

A Final Word on Wood Cleaners

While I don't believe the chlorinated cleaners are the best in all cases, it is the only way I know of to effectively and economically _sterilize_ a wood surface. You may not think your wood needs to be sterilized, but most wood finishes just don't contain enough fungicide in them to kill existing colonies of mildew. These colonies may not even be visible to the eye, since they are microscopic and are only visible when there are billions of them concentrated in a small area. But, if there are microscopic mold spores on the wood, and you apply a finish, the mold could continue to grow despite fungicide additives in the stain. This could create a more difficult time removing the mold since you would first have to remove the stain, bleach the mold to kill it, then try to match up the treated area to the rest of the house. If your house logs were not treated with a fungicide just prior to leaving the log yard, or they have been on your site more than a few weeks and if your climate will support mildew organisms, it's a good idea to spray the house down with a bleach treatment and rinse well prior to applying a long term wood finish. Bleach has no residual features and will not prevent mold from coming back. It only kills mold with about 10 minutes of contact, so don't wait more than a week or two before finishing your logs.

Chapter Nine
Pressure Washing

A good cleaning will most likely require the use of power tools. First we'll give an overview of pressure washing. Pressure washing will remove the top layer of wood fibers, as well as a failing finish. It is a good idea to pressure wash after you have used your cleaners and strippers. A pressure washer is a machine that takes water from your water hose and pumps it through a smaller high pressure hose to a wand with a trigger, then through a very tiny opening called the tip. Pressure washer tips control the width of the fan of water that you spray. For example, a 15 degree tip will produce a fan of high pressure water about 6" wide when it is held about 12" from the surface of the wood. A 45 degree tip, will produce a fan about 14" wide.

You can rent a pressure washer at most rental companies and paint stores. There are three features to look for in a pressure washer:

1. A gas powered motor
2. A pump with a minimum flow rate of 3 gallons per minute
3. A rating of about 2000-2500 psi

Most machines at rental yards meet these parameters.

There are two areas of concern when using a pressure washer. One is getting water <u>in</u> the house and the other is <u>damaging the</u>

wood surface. Here are some things you can do to minimize, or at least deal with both situations.

As mentioned earlier, if the log home has leaks that you know of, caulk those areas and let the caulk cure before you pressure wash. Otherwise, you may not be able to use a pressure washer, since the leaks would permit lots of water to come into your home. If you suspect that you may have a problem with air leaks, but don't know exactly where they are, you will find out when you pressure wash the house. I've never seen or heard of a log home being pressure washed that didn't have at least <u>some</u> water coming through either the corners, grain checks, around doors and windows or lateral seals, but Don't Worry! Have someone on the inside with towels, plastic and a wet vac if necessary. Make a note of where the leaks are, and make sure that they get sealed. If the leaks are severe, you may consider removing any water color paintings from the walls, covering the furniture or any other precautions that you deem necessary.

A pressure washer can destroy the looks and integrity of a wood surface if not used properly, so if you've never used a pressure washer, here's a few tips on proper techniques. Weathered wood has lost much of the lignin on the surface, and

Notice the clean logs that have been pressure washed, versus the logs that have not.

you will probably see some tiny fibers appear after you pressure wash. Fuzzy wood can be extensive, but can be minimized if you are careful about what you are doing and avoid using excessive pressure.

Tips to Avoid Damaging the Wood

Ideally, you want a flow rate of about 4 gallons per minute, but don't use a machine rated over 3000 psi. Pressures higher than that can do more harm than good on soft wood.

• Pressure washers usually come with a few tip sizes which can determine how wide the spray pattern will be. A zero degree tip will spray a stream that will damage the wood and will pierce the skin. A 15 degree fan is OK if you've got some experience with pressure washers, but for the first timer, it's still too much

Notice the fuzzy appearance of the wood, caused from improper pressure washing.

for soft wood. Usually, a 25 to 45 degree fan is adequate for log homes, but be careful not to damage the wood. If the wood gets a fuzzy appearance, you're over doing it. Use the largest tip size that you can and back away from the surface a little more.

• The pressure is rated at the pump head, so if you have 100 feet of hose, the pressure drops by about 2 psi per foot or more, especially if the washer is downhill from the project you are washing.

.• The third way to avoid damaging the wood is to reduce the idle speed of the motor, which reduces the pressure.

• The fourth way to avoid damage, is to keep the spray farther away from the wood. With old wood, you should not have the tip any closer than 18" from the wood surface. If you have the tip any closer, you'll damage the wood for sure. Some pressure washers come with a dual lance wand with a pressure adjustment right on the handle. This is very similar to an over and under shotgun, whereby the top barrel will have a normal spray tip and the bottom will have one about four times larger, that can be closed or opened by the user. Then part of the flow bypasses the high pressure nozzle.

• A common occurrence with the first timers is pressure marks all over the place. There are two causes of presssure marks: Holding the wand close to the wood when you first pull the trigger, and holding the wand too long in one place.

When you first pull the trigger, aim the wand away from the wood for the initial blast, then make your pass. You should make abour three or four passes over the same area in about 5 seconds. In other words, pressure washing is a very active sport. Keep the wand moving quickly at all times.

Many factors including tip size, water pressure and how far back you hold the wand will effect your results.

• NEVER, NEVER point a pressure washer at your skin, foot or at anyone else. It can penetrate the skin and cause extreme pain and expensive medical bills.

Chapter Ten
Sandblasting

Another option for getting your wood ready for refinishing is sandblasting. In some cases sandblasting may be necessary to get the old finish off. Wet sand is usually more gentle than dry sand. In some cases, pressure washers can be rigged up with a sand pot and hose that draws sand into the water stream. Also, sand comes in various particle sizes, from fine to course. The object is, to get off the finish without damaging the wood, so start with the smallest particle size you can. Leave the large particle sand to the guys that sandblast the barnacles off submarines.

Logs pictured above have been sandblasted to remove old stain. Although the logs are clean and ready for new finish, there appears to be some damage to the wood.

I once saw a house in Montana being sandblasted. As I drove by, I noticed a huge cloud of dust and went back to take a closer look. Evidently, the former home owners, in a last ditch effort to keep the cold Montana winter out of their house, had applied about a 6 inch layer of spray foam to the entire exterior of the home. They covered the logs with this foam and then painted them black. The place looked like a giant ice chest. When the house was sold, the new owners decided to re-expose the logs and had the whole place sandblasted. It worked! After a generous coat of stain and large quantities of chinking, they have a warm and cozy log home. However, the sandblasting pitted the logs pretty badly.

Chapter Eleven
Chemical Strippers

In some cases, cleaners and pressure washing may not be enough to get your logs ready for a finish. In some instances chemical strippers may be needed.

The old standby strippers have always contained methylene chloride. This ingredient has caused cancer in lab rats and is suspected carcinogenic in humans. Strippers containing methylene chloride are on the Environmental Protection Agency's hit list, just as Penta-containing wood preservatives were a few years ago. Mehylene Chloride is being phased out of strippers and will be illegal in most states by the end of 1996.

A stripper is used when there is a film of stain or preservative on the logs that is visible, and will inhibit the adhesion or penetration of a new coat. Linseed oil that has been applied in multiple coats will build a film as well as other finishes, both water borne and solvent borne. The stripper's job is to dissolve or melt the film. It usually takes from one hour to one day to do so, depending upon how thick the film is. Regardless of how long it takes, once the film is melted--you have to get it off before it dries and reattaches itself to the wood. The easiest way to do this, is with a pressure washer. Do a small test area first. After applying the stripper, take a paint brush and see if you can move the film. Once it is soft enough to move and if you can see bare wood underneath, then drag out the power washer and go to it. However, if the log walls leak, you will have to get rid of the dissolved finish by hand. This can be done with a long handled brush and a water hose. Be careful when dealing with strippers. They are designed to melt paint and can cause severe burns on your skin, as well as eye damage which may range from strong irritation to blindness.

Once you finish stripping the project, you may or may not have good looking wood. If the stripper removed 80 or 90% of the old finish, it was a success. Sanding will most likely be necessary on stubborn spots. Also, many strippers will create fuzzy logs that may need a light sanding to get them smooth again. If the stripping process darkened the wood, then you should give the logs an application of an oxalic acid based cleaner. In most cases this will neutralize the stripper and bring the pH of the wood back to normal. As we already discussed, after you get the oxalic acid on the wood, wait about 15 minutes and give it a good rinsing with a power washer, using a fairly large tip size. Don't waste your time with a water hose and jet nozzle. If you've gone this far to restore your wood, don't cut corners to save a few bucks. If you do it right the first time, and maintain the home at regular intervals, you may never have to do this again.

This bridge, in it's scenic setting features wood in it's natural, unstained form. Left unprotected, it will turn dark and dingy, requiring restoration.

A stripper usually works better on a failing finish than a new one. A new generation of strippers has already emerged that contain either dibasic ester (DBE) or N-methyl pyrrolidione (NMP). They are safer, but take longer to work. There are some strippers that you can let dry and peel off like dried glue from the palms of third graders. There are other strippers emerging every day, so shop around. Also, you may find one that works really well on most of the house, but not on all of it. Don't hesitate to try a different stripper, even one that has methylene chloride in it. However, only use it outside and protect your eyes and skin, and avoid working so close to the wood that you are breathing fumes. Whichever type of stripper you use, it is usually a good idea to wet down all shrubs, plants and grass before application. Cover them with plastic and then rinse them well afterwards.

Chapter Twelve
Wood Preservatives

To preserve wood, means to prevent wood destroying organisms from attacking the wood. The corner notches and lateral notches are especially vulnerable since water can get trapped inside, creating a moist environment.

I once saw a log home that appeared to be solid, but because of poor drainage and no roof overhang on one end of the house, the logs were completely rotten. The outer inch or so was solid wood, but behind that, you could reach into the log and grab handfuls of wood compost. Water seeped down between the logs and collected there. It never really dried out and rot set in, which attracted more moisture. Consequently, the whole side of this two story home had to be replaced.

Notice the rot in the third log.

Products that use the language "wood preservative" are required to be registered with the EPA. Also, if the label claims to control any kind of biological activity, it has to be registered as well. Just because a product has an EPA registration number does not mean it's going to kill you.

The EPA neither approves nor tests products for quality. Their job is to have full documentation on every chemical in the market that claims to kill living organisms, or prevent organisms from living. In the EPA's position, if it says it can kill something, they have to know what it is, and the environmental impact it will have if a truckload of it crashes and ends up in the river. Therefore, the term "wood preservative" should not be used casually for wood finishes, unless the product is actually registered with the EPA.

Some stain manufacturers are using a technique called "green marketing". They use scare tactics to try to create chemical phobias in the minds of the public. *Non toxic* has become more of a marketing buzz word, than a description. There is nothing you can put on a log home to prevent rot or insects from attacking it, that does not have some degree of toxicity to plants and insects. That does not mean it is toxic to mammals. Don't fall into the trap that by using a "non toxic" product, you will be saving the earth. If it is truly non toxic, it will probably not protect your wood from decay. However, rest assured, the highly toxic paint additives that were once used, are not even available today. The ones used in today's materials are much more specific as to their toxicity, and much less toxic to organisms outside the target.

As long as these products are used in accordance with label instructions and precautions are taken against ingestion and skin/eye contact,

With no gutters, the rain spills off the roof, hits the dirt and splashes up on the logs. Mold is growing in the first stage of decay.

you really should not hesitate to use them. Remember, nature is trying to return your wood to the earth. You must interrupt this process and postpone it. You can do so without destroying yourself or the earth.

Here is a list of common wood preservatives, all of which are registered with the EPA.

First, is an explanation of what I consider industrial wood preservatives: *They are only used by forest products companies and require several hundred thousand dollars of equipment for their use.*

These beautiful, large logs are not being used to their best potential. The logs that stick out past the roof will be accesible to water damage. The roof overhangs are not adequate and the roof itself leaves a lot of room for further damage.

• *CCA*

Also known as "wolmanized" or pressure treated wood, or just treated wood. CCA is Chromated Copper Arsenate. It is sold as a concentrate and used in the pressure treating process. Wood treated with CCA turns a green color unless a brown pigment is added to it, like is done on the west coast. CCA treatments are available for house logs through a handful of suppliers, but the green color is a real turnoff. However, the green color will eventually fade to gray after several months. CCA is used extensively in treating utility poles, marine pilings, decking materials and landscape timbers. It is a waterborne solution, so less porous wood species need to be incised to increase penetration.

• *Pentachlorophenol*

Penta is still around and is used to treat utility poles. It was never banned, it just became a restricted use pesticide, meaning that it could only be used by certified applicators in industrial settings. Due to penta's smell and toxicity, it is not used in log homes. However, before it became a restricted use pesticide, it was available over the counter. Several products contained penta, and for a long time they were used on log homes. It is a very effective pesticide, insecticide, fungicide and mildewcide. However, it smells really bad, and has killed several lab rats.

• *Creosote*

Creosote is made from coal tar and petroleum distillates. It is used extensively to treat utility poles and railroad crossties. It never really dries and it adds flexibility to heavy timbers. It is used in a pressure treating vessel. The timbers are treated green (unseasoned) and steam conditioned as part of the 24 hour process. Due to it's smell and toxicity, it is not used in log homes.

There are few other industrial preservatives on the market, but the main three above make up more than 90% of the industrial wood preserving industry.

• *Borates*

Borates have been used as wood preservatives for over 40 years in Europe, Australia and New Zealand. They are effective against all major wood destroying organism including: fungal decay, termites, beetles and rot. Borates have no smell or color, making them quite suitable for log homes. They are among the safest wood preservatives available today. Their use in North America has increased dramatically since the late 1980's. The dry borate powder has roughly half the toxicity to mammals as table salt.

One of the unique features of borate treatments is it it's ability to diffuse through wood. Diffusion is the way the product spreads itself out in the wood, much the same way as an open bottle of ammonia would spread itself out in a small room. However, since borates are dry, they have to be in liquid form to diffuse through wood. This is usually accomplished by putting them in a solution of water or glycol.

Generally, house logs must have a fairly high moisture content in order to get borate diffusion to take place. Imagine each borate molecule as a tiny canoe. It doesn't need an ocean to make it mobile, just a little creek will do, but no amount of paddling will get you down a dirt road in a canoe. The same is true with borates. The wetter the wood, the easier it is for the borates to diffuse. However, treating relatively dry wood is still a good idea. If the wood ever gets wet enough to rot, the borates will become mobile and move to the damper areas and prevent decay from occurring. Borate treatments are generally a one time deal. The key to avoiding reapplications is to keep a water repellent finish on the wood, and keeping the wood out of contact with the soil or running water.

Borates work differently on different wood-destroying organisms. They have been proven very effective in combating termites. Termites do not actually digest wood, the have microscopic protozoa in their intestines that digest the wood. The termite survives on the by-products from the protozoa. When the termite has a diet consisting of borate treated wood, the borates kill the protozoa that the termite needs to survive and the termite starves to death.

For some insects, borates in wood act as an abrasive and causes dehydration. The sharp edges on the borate crystals scratches the waxy exoskeleton which causes major fluid loss. Other insects that ingest borate treated wood die from either dehydration or a disruption of their metabolic processes.

For decay fungi or rot, borates act as a contact poison and kills them. However, borates are not very effective against mold and mildew. These are different organisms, and other products are necessary to protect against them.

Take note of the beetle hole, with signs of activity. Borate treatments are known for combatting beetles, as well as other insects.

Chapter Thirteen
Borates

Traditional borate treatments have utilized a dip tank, whereby <u>green or unseasoned logs</u> are submerged for several minutes in a heated solution, about 125 degrees of about 25-30% disodium octaborate tetrahydrate. Then they are moved to a drip pad, where runoff is recaptured and reused. The logs are then covered with plastic for a few weeks while the diffusion process takes place. As long as green logs are used, one can expect several inches of borate diffusion using this method.

In the last few years two products have emerged for spray-on borate treatment. These products are very useful when the home is already built, and there is rot or bugs present. They are also used as a precautionary treatment, but the logs must be bare. As with traditional treatments, the logs need to be wet enough to allow diffusion to take place. Otherwise the borates will remain just under the wood's surface.

There are currently two types of spray applied borate treatments.

• *Timbor or Penetreat*
Timbor or Penetreat is a dry white powder that is mixed with water and applied to the wood using either spray, brush, injection or dip treatment. Normally you would use one pound of powder per gallon of water to make a 10% solution. Two coats are gener-

ally required. This solution is sprayed or brushed onto the wood. It should not be done on a hot windy day, or in direct sunlight. Otherwise, the water will evaporate away too quickly, leaving white powder or crystals on the surface. Nor should it be done on a rainy day or when rain is imminent and there is a chance the treatment will get washed off. Also, you should plan on doing two applications a day apart.

When spraying these borate treatments, make sure you get some solution between each log. Go heavy on the log ends, door and window openings and corners. These areas are more porous, and therefore more vulnerable to rot. This is also an excellent solution to squirt into checks that have opened up in your logs. I would fill each check, then allow it to soak in. After a few hours, or even the next day, fill each check again, then caulk or chink it to prevent water from collecting in it. Using hot water will allow you to add twice as much powder, which will make the solution twice as strong.   However, the chance for crystallization on the surface goes way up, and so this stronger solution should only be used for checks and other areas that will not be seen. Also, as the temperature cools, borates will fall out of the solution, which may clog your sprayer, so the idea is to use it quickly then, rinse your sprayer thoroughly.

• *Bora-Care or Boracol*

Bora-Care or Boracol is a 40% concentration of Timbor. It is a liquid glycol solution that helps to promote diffusion quicker and deeper in dryer wood. As purchased, it is a concentrate that is thinned with water. The concentrate has the consistency of honey. Use a gallon of hot water for every gallon of Bora-Care or Boracol. When you first start mixing it, you will think that it will never get thinner, but keep mixing and when you think you have it, mix it some more. If not mixed completely, it will clog spray equipment, so make sure you mix the heck out of it. Also, you have to use the mixed solution that day. The pot life is about 12 hours, once the concentrate is diluted. Rinse your equipment well and pump clean water through it to clear the lines.

While more expensive, research has indicated that Bora-Care or Boracol is more effective at controlling certain wood destroying organisms. It can be used in the same application as discussed, for Timbor or Penetreat, with much less chance of residue on the surface.

Regardless of the spray borate treatment you use, you will only be treating the outer 2" or less, unless the wood is *very* wet. Even if you were only able to treat the outer 1/2" of a new home, built with good solid logs and no pockets of decay, I believe that you would have a well protected log home. Borates are not "fixed preservatives". They mobilize whenever the wood's moisture content is high enough to support decay fungi. Therefore, if you get checks in you logs and water gets in them and wets the wood below the surface, the borates migrate there with the moisture of the wood.

If you get some residue or crystals forming on the surface a few days after borate treatment, mist them down with water and they will most likely redissolve and go into the wood. Do NOT stain over the crystals unless you want to see them forever. If you have to stain right now, and there are crystals on the surface, remove them with a dry broom or brush.

A borate solution was applied to dry wood on a dry day, in direct sunlight. It dried on the surface, before it had a chance to soak in.

• *Impel Rods*

Impel Rods are a solid form of the borate preservative whose use originated in Europe several decades ago. They come in diameters of either 1/2" or 3/4", and lengths of either 3" or 4". They are inserted into holes that you drill deep into the logs that either have rot or have the potential for rot. When the moisture reaches about 30%, they begin to dissolve, releasing the highest concentration of borate preservative available. Each rod will treat an area of about one cubic foot. It is a good idea to use Impel Rods in combination with the other borate preservatives as an "internal log treatment", since spraying the logs with either borate solution only treat the outer shell of the log. If your house is more than a few years old and you have some suspicious areas, with telltale signs of water damage and organic growth, I highly recommend a combination of internal and external treatments.

This structure is covered with black mold. Notice that the roof overhang terminates at the logs. This design offers no protection to the logs from water.

If you suspect you may have a problem, you first have to determine the location of the rot. Telltale signs of wet wood are the first clue. Tap around the area with a hammer and listen for the difference between the resonant tone of solid wood versus the dull thud of rotten wood. Also, inspect around large checks and areas around doors and windows. Monitor corners and log ends, especially if they protrude beyond the eaves. If you find some areas where you suspect rot, Don't Worry! Rot is like a cancer that will continue to spread, but it can be cured with a good dose of borates. I suggest drilling about 3/4" holes, as deep as you can without punching through to the other side of the log, then filling those areas with the liquid borate solution. The solution will seep in rather quickly, so fill up those holes 4 or 5 times, then insert a couple of solid borate rods. Plug the hole with treated wood dowels, caulk or chinking. Do this in a couple of areas where the rot is, and then about 12-18" on either side. Also treat the logs above and below the area, then spray the whole area with borate solution.

There is a lot of research going on now, and promising results have been indicated using various surface applied borate solutions with favorable results. However, since borate treatments are not locked into the wood, they can leak out. Therefore, *the key to any borate treatment is to keep a water repellent finish on your logs.* When it stops repelling water, and the logs get wet, the borates come to the surface and could get washed out of the wood. If your home is borate treated, make sure your water repellent is repelling water. Borate solutions can only be applied to bare wood. If your logs have a water repellent finish on them, it must be removed prior to borate treating.

Chapter Fourteen
Anti-Sapstain Fungicides

T hese are products that protect wood against mold and mildew in the log yard, overseas container, sawmill or job site. They should be applied within 24 hours after the logs have been peeled or machined if the log yard is in an area where mold is a problem. These fungicides normally do not have a binder, no resins, or anything to make them a long term product, but they serve an important function in keeping mold and mildew from growing on freshly cut house logs. If your house logs are delivered to your site, and it will be several weeks, or months until you apply the long term stain or preservative, and if you are in area where mold is a concern, then you can give your home a pretreatment with an anti-sapstain fungicide.

Some common preservatives used in yard fungicides are:

• *Copper Napthenate*
Copper Napthenate is approved for ground contact. It is often used as a butt treatment for fence posts. It gives the wood a distinctive bright green color which fades to light brown.

• *Copper 8 Quinolinolate*
Copper 8 Quinolinolate is a very safe product approved by the FDA for treatment of wooden food storage bins and pallets that come in contact with food. When diluted to the recommended dosages, it does not cause significant color changes.

71

• *Chlorothalanil*

Chlorothalanil is another very safe product that is used as a herbicide on food crops. It is very effective in controlling mold and mildew, but hard to keep in solution. This product can also cause skin sensitivity.

• *Busan*

Busan offers very effective control of mold, mildew, sapstain and decay, but has a very foul odor.

• *Polyphase*

Polyphase is a fairly new product that has had a great deal of success replacing Penta in spray or dip applications in sawmills. It has very little odor and a low mammalian toxicity. It does not discolor the wood and is available in several different products.

Chapter Fifteen
Wood Finishes

Proper use of wood finishes determine the color of the home, protect the wood's surface and address local conditions such as moisture and high altitude sunlight. People spend more time and energy selecting a wood species than the product they select to protect the wood. There are many subtle differences in wood species, but in the long run, the difference is fairly insignificant. The way the logs fit together, how the home is designed and how the wood is protected from Mother Nature, are far more important than the wood species. Log builders generally use the best wood they can get at a reasonable price. They develop the optimum log building systems for that type of wood. Potential log home owners waste a lot of time on selecting a wood species and end up buying the cheapest stuff they can find to protect it. What you do to your wood, and how you take care of it, is a continual process and far outweighs the species of wood.

Wood finishes are known as water repellent preservatives, water repellents, wood preservatives, natural finishes, transparent stains, semitransparent stains, ultra-transparent stains and architectural coatings. Whatever you call them, they can be broadly divided into four categories: **House Paint, Solid Colored Stains, Semi Transparent Stains and Ultra Transparent Stains.** Each of these types of finishes can be either oil based or water based.

Since very few log homes get painted, I will not spend much time on paints. Most log homes get finished with ultra transparent[1] finishes or natural finishes. There are five basic types of wood finishes available for log homes today. Unfortunately, <u>transparent finishes offer the least amount of protection from the sun's harmful ultraviolet radiation.</u> They usually contain water repellents and biocides for added protection, but since the level of tint is usually relatively low, they need to be maintained much more frequently than the more opaque finishes and paints.

Clear Wood Finishes

Almost every log home owner I've ever talked to wants a *"CLEAR"* finish on their logs. For the purpose of this discussion I'm going to say that *"CLEAR"* means a finish or preservative that has no pigment, dye or tint and does not change the color of the wood. In the lacquer industry they call it water white. Owners of new log homes don't want to change the color at all. They've been looking at these beautiful blond naked logs for months and have bonded with them. Now, they know they need to protect them, but they don't want to change the color. Well, unfortunately, it can't be done. Sunlight causes the wood to darken or turn gray. Mold and mildew grow and turn the wood black in spots. Dirt and airborne pollutants settle on the logs and within a few months, unprotected wood changes colors by itself and the blond look is gone. Therefore, if you don't change the color with a high quality wood finish, Mother Nature will do it her way.

Unless the entire home is built in the trees and is shaded all day, all year, in an area where snow cover won't reflect light onto the logs, it is necessary to use a pigmented wood finish to protect it from the sun's harmful effects. The pigmentation provides most

---

[1]Some finishes are totally clear or "Water White". These are <u>*not*</u> recommended at all for log homes, since there is virtually no UV protection which causes more problems. Ultra transparent refers to lightly tinted finishes that impart some coloration to the wood while still allowing the grain to show through.

of the UV protection in any transparent finish by filtering, reflecting and refracting light rays before they get to the wood surface. The higher level of pigments, the more UV protections the finish offers. However, high pigment levels do not necessarily mean the product is real dark.

Some stain manufactures add UV absorbers and inhibitors to their finish. There are many different types. Most of these ingredients are *sacrificial* in that they take the hit from the sun, first collecting hydrogen atoms produced by thermal reactions in the wood's molecular level. However, they can only hold back a certain amount of solar radiation and so once they're full, they no longer serve a purpose. These are the same types of ingredients used in suntan lotions, but they last longer. The type of UV absorbers and UV inhibitors used in transparent finished are very expensive.

Nonpenetrating oil stains may peel similar to paint without the proper protection.

Photo Courtesy of the Exterior Wood in the South Publication

In order for them to be optimized, there must be a film "after the finish is dry" at least 2 mills thick. Otherwise, long term UV protection is impossible. However, as paint technology advances and when the market is willing to pay a higher price for it, I am convinced there will some day be clear finishes that protect the wood from UV light. <u>Until then, be very skeptical of anyone trying to sell you a penetrating clear finish that protects the wood from UV damage.</u>

Pigments and Tints

Pigments and tints used in the paint and stain industry come in different particle sizes. Just as an espresso grind for coffee takes more grinding time than a coarser grind for a percolator, the smaller the particle size, the more expensive it is because it has to go through a more extensive grinding process. A paint manufacturer can get by with large particle sized pigments because the wood surface is totally hidden by an opaque film. However, wood stains that use traditional paint pigments only use a minute amount in order to keep the color as light as possible. This method keeps the cost per gallon down, but does not offer the best UV protection for your wood. A quality oriented stain manufacturer will use a much smaller particle size and add a bunch of it to his product. The smaller particle size does not obscure the transparency of the finish, and provides far superior protection from the sun's harmful effects. Another thing the finish manufacturer can do to boost it's performance is to add a combination of UV absorbers and inhibitors to the product.

A natural wood finish should be maintained whenever there are visible signs that the wood is aging. Examples are discoloration between the top and bottom of a log on the sunny side of the house, or when the wood no longer beads water. This should be part of a walk around inspection of your home several times per year. See the inspection checklist included in this book for these, and several other points to consider.

Solids

Solids are what's left behind after the finish dries. They include things like tint, resins, binders, wax, fungicides, mildewcides, UV absorbers and inhibitors, non drying oils and pigments.

Cheap or Economical?

Some nationally advertised products you see on TV commercials contain less than 10% solids. So 90% of the product can evaporates in a few short hours, so if you buy 10 gallons of that material, over 9 gallons of solvents evaporate into the atmosphere and less than one gallon is distributed over the entire area that you spent the better part of your Saturday afternoon "treating".

At $8.00 per gallon for the cheap stuff, that's $80.00 worth of material for the equivalent of about 1 gallon of solids. That's the equivilent of $80.00 per gallon. A good product contains at least 40% solids and the really good products contain 60-70% solids. Let's say the cheap product is called Tom's Water Seal. For $80.00, you get the equivalent of about 1 gallon of solids. Let's say the good stuff is called Tim's Wood Preservative and contains 50% solids, but costs $32.00 per gallon or 4 times more per gallon than the cheap stuff. Buying 2 gallons of Tim's gives you the equivalent of 1 gallon of solids and costs you $64.00. Compare that to Tom's at $80.00 for the same amount of solids. Now, which product is more economical? Both require the same application procedures, but to get the equivalent protection you would have to apply 5 gallons of Tom's for every 1 gallon of Tim's.

The price tag on the can may be cheap, but when you consider that 90% of the product disappears and has no lasting effect on the wood, then it becomes a very expensive product. A product with less than 10% solids will not last more than a few months. Solids are what you pay for. Everything else included are just vehicles to get the solids in or on the wood.

Volatile Organic Compounds

VOC's are the stuff like paint thinner and glycol that *volatilize*, and are theoretically responsible for ozone depletion. California, New York, Texas and Arizona have already passed strict laws governing the levels of VOC's in a product. Many common stains and finishes cannot be sold in those states, at least not legally. There is talk now of federal standards which would regulate all of the states, beginning in the year 2003.

There are five basic types of transparent wood finishes:

• *Solvent Borne Systems*

These are probably the most common type of products on the market today. There are good ones and bad ones, but in general, they are between 5 and 30% solids. Make sure if you use one of these products, it contains a mold/mildew control, a color (don't use *"CLEAR"*) and plan on maintaining it as soon as it stops beading water or loses some of it's color. These products need to be applied most frequently, but the good ones will last 3-5 years.

• *Film Building Resins*

These are usually multi-coat systems that form a thick film on the wood. These are very tough systems and should only be applied to well seasoned wood. They are usually glossy in appearance and when applied correctly and not exposed to intense sunlight, these systems can last longer than most other transparent finishes. They normally completely encapsulate the wood's surface and have been known to stop water transportation through knots.

However, as we've learned, moisture in wood is primarily transported longitudinally, not radially. Therefore, most of the moisture is lost through the log ends and checks. Having said that, I have seen cases where an inflexible film has broken down as pockets of moisture form beneath

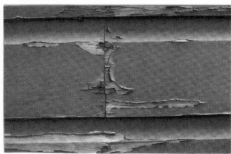

A film can peel or flake if the wood is too moist when treated, or when the film is not perodically maintained.

Photo Courtesy of the Exterior Wood
in the South Publication

78

the film and causes an adhesive failure. In full sun, some of these systems could be subject to cracking in 2 to 3 years when not maintained. Some completely seal the wood and have been known to stop water infiltration through knots. Some resinous systems are not breathable and should not be applied to green or unseasoned logs without some sort of weathering or wood conditioning product first. A resinous film needs to be flexible enough to give with the dimensional changes of the wood and allow vapor transmission through it from within the log.

• *Oil Emulsions*

These systems have been around since the early 1980's. They are hybrid systems that contain varying quantities of oils or solvents, but have an additive in them that allows them to mix together in water. This additive is called a surfactant. Soap is the most common surfactant. Think about it, soap allows the grease on your hands to mix with the water from your faucet and be rinsed away. Who says oil and water don't mix? Surfactants are used in a multitude of chemicals and cosmetics and pharmaceuticals.

Most oil emulsions contain latex polymers, alkyd resins and linseed oil. Their performance varies from product to product, but it is very difficult to get total transparency with any of them. Oil emulsions are more common in VOC compliant states where the manufacturers have tried to reduce emissions by replacing the solvents with water. There is a fairly delicate balance in many of these formulas and thinning with water or solvent is not recommended. Also you need to use copious amounts of soap (a surfactant or emulsifier) because the water and oil separate and it is very difficult to clean up. Usually the soap and water cleanup needs to be followed with solvent cleanup, such as paint thinner or mineral spirits.

• *Latex Stains*

These systems build a very light surface film that does allow moisture to pass through it, so they can be applied to wetter wood. They are polymer based and create a breathable, flexible, water repellent film. Cleanup is usually fast and complete with soap and water.

These finishes have a potential to soften when exposed to lots of rain and should never be used on horizontal surfaces like decks, rails or cedar roofs. It is also difficult to maintain these finishes, since in time they lose their transparency and need to be removed before recoating with anything else. Also, they are difficult to strip since latex polymers don't dissolve with traditional strippers. Make sure you use a stripper that is recommended for latexes when stripping one of these finishes.

• *Penetrating Oil Finishes*

The latest technology in oil based preservatives utilize paraffinic oils, which are UV resistant, do not oxidize, and are VOC compliant. These new types of oil based finishes are generally more expensive than most solvent or water borne systems. They are low in odor and have performed extremely well in outdoor exposure tests for wood protection and color retention. On heavily sun damaged wood, most oil based preservatives are very effective in rebulking the wood fibers and replacing the oils that were lost, adding lubricity to the wood. I have seen small surface checks actually close up after a few days of treatment with a high solids oil finish. Splintering is also significantly reduced.

Top: A window which was treated with a penetrating water repellent wood preservative. Bottom: A window that was not pretreated and is already showing paint flaking and chipping.
Photo Courtesy of the Exterior Wood in the South Publication

• "Natural" Oil Based Products

Natural oils are oils derived from non-petroleum sources. Examples of natural oils are vegetable oils, linseed oil and rosewood oil. Since these oils are "natural", they all contain large quantities of nutrients which mold and mildew spores often use as a food source. I have never seen one of these "natural oil" based products in use over two years that didn't have a large degree of organic growth. As a matter of fact, I have seen projects that turned black from mildew in less than one year. The only way to prevent these products from becoming mildew fertilizer, is by adding mercurial or pentachlorophenol based fungicides to them, which have been outlawed by the EPA. My advice is to stay away from them unless you are in a very arid part of the country and you can inspect a project over two years old that has been treated with the product you are considering.

Chapter Sixteen
Application of Wood Finishes

As mentioned earlier, always read the label instructions before undertaking a finishing project. Call the supplier if you have any further questions. Follow their recommendations, but keep an open mind. Instructions are written to cover 80% of the situations. There may be exceptions to the rules and there may be situations that aren't covered in the instructions. Below are a few pointers that are known as general rules of thumb.

If the finish you are using can be sprayed, the label will state it. However, stay away from inexpensive pump up hand sprayers, unless you are doing a very small project, like a picnic table or small deck. Rent a professional spray rig at your local equipment rental yard. The job will be easier and it will look better. $25.00 pump sprayers are OK for applying wood cleaners, and spraying weed killers, but don't waste your time trying to stain your log home with one. Also, plan on back-brushing to insure uniform coverage and to catch any runs or drips.

• If you are unfamiliar with the spray equipment or the products you are using, don't start painting at the front door. Use an old piece of plywood or scraps of wood to get the feel of the equipment. Then start at the back of the house. If you rent the equipment, ask for a demonstration on spraying as well as cleaning the tip and troubleshooting equipment problems.

• If the temperature is at the cooler end of the recommended painting temperatures, store the products inside a heated home the night before you use it. This will keep it from cooling to the nighttime temperature outside, then thickening to the point where they are difficult to spray.

• If temperatures are at the warmer end of the recommended painting temperatures, avoid painting in direct sunlight. The finish usually needs to be wet for 30-60 minutes on the wood for proper film formation and penetration. If it's 90 degrees outside, the wall temperature could be 130 degrees or more. This could interfere with the product's adhesion and penetration. Ideal temperatures for most wood finishes is between 60 and 80 degrees. However, staining should not take place below 40 degrees or above 90 degrees.

• Relative humidity is an important temperature. If the humidity is less than 30%, your application temperature can be as low as 40 degrees. Don't even start the job if you're going to try to stain your house between thunderstorms. Wait until you're relatively sure you will have a dry day. Slightly overcast is better than full sun. Also, don't start the job until last night's dew is off the wood, and don't start the job in the late afternoon when dew or fog is expected that night.

• Whether the product is pigmented or not, it will need to be mixed thoroughly before and during use. The good stuff will be stuck to the bottom of the can, so empty each container into an empty container. Then take a paint brush and wipe he bottom of the can with a little of the recommended thinner. Then pour the contents back and forth several times to mix it completely. Stir your mixture every half hour or so to keep it uniformly mixed.

• Mask everything that you don't want sprayed. Paint sprayers atomize products so fine that air currents can carry them several feet from where you are spraying. Buy a roll of plastic and cover the lawn furniture, shrubs, concrete, grass and anything else that you don't want stained. Mask windows, doors, exterior lights and any trim or wood that will get coated with a different color. Move your cars upwind a few hundred feet.

• Never spray your hand to test the pressure. The finish could be forced into your skin causing blood poisoning or other problems.

• Always wear a dust mask or respirator when spraying wood finishes. Use eye and skin protection and wash your hands thoroughly before eating, smoking or using the bathroom.

• Use common sense on ladders. Don't overextend your reach. Move the ladder to the next place you have to work. Keep metal ladders away from power lines. Always set ladders on dry level ground. On hillsides, dig out a place so the ladder feet can rest flat. Use a heavy duty ladder whenever possible. Look for a wood ladder with a wire rung under each wood rung. Never stand on the top two or three rungs, and never stand on the fold out paint shelf. Hook your paint can to the ladder to keep it from falling.

• Rent scaffolding if ladder work is too cumbersome. It comes with wheels so it can be moved around the house with relative ease. Scaffolding will provide you with a 4 foot by 10 foot working platform and will make for relatively easy work. Hint: Assemble one end first, then the two sides, then the other end. After that assemble the crossbar and platform. Don't assemble the wheels until you have the first section complete. Lock the wheels down tight and follow the same procedure for the second tier.

• Clean your tools and equipment immediately after you finish the job. The longer you wait, the more difficult the job will be. Solvent based thinners can be reused several times. When completely done, let them evaporate, then take the remainder to a paint recycler or dispose of it in accordance with local regulations.

• Spray at least a gallon of solvent through the system when you have finished for the day. Solvent is defined as whatever is recommended for cleanup on the label. Usually it is either water or paint thinner.

How is quality defined?

There are many factors that go into the equation of quality such as ease of application, resistance to fading, durability, mildew resistance, cleanup and overall aesthetic appeal. You cannot tell much by reading the brochures since they all say essentially the same thing, because they are all supposed to do the same thing.

Jenny Craig Corporate Headquarters in San Diego, California. The beams were black and grungy. They were stripped, pressure washed and treated with TWP.

86

However, price is usually a fairly good indicator of quality when it comes to paints and stains. Don't waste your money on anything that sells for around $10.00 per gallon. Mid range price for a decent wood finish is around $20.00 per gallon. Upper end high quality finishes sell for around $30.00 per gallon. However, beware of products that sell for over $50.00 per gallon. They may be good quality, but the value received may not be worth the price tag.

Make sure that the person you buy the product from, can explain the application nuances and give you tips that aren't necessarily right off the label instructions. Don't be afraid to ask for references of other customers that have used the product on a log home, preferably in your area. I haven't found one single product that works perfectly for every application in every section of the country, regardless of the weather conditions. There are several products out there that make those claims. A product used for a deck in the hot, dry climate of Arizona, should be quite different in chemical makeup than a product made for a log home in the cool, damp Pacific Northwest, or for fences in the extremes of the

Mid-West or siding in the hot and muggy summers of Florida.

As a general rule, the higher the solids content, the higher the quality. Thorough and realistic label instructions are another indication that the manufacturer is on their toes. Independent testing is one of the best ways to gain a comfort level with the product. Chances are, you won't be able to get the actual test procedures and conclusions, but a letter or article about the product, from a researcher, or even a professional painter, will give you confidence in the product.

While on the issue of testing, most paint and stain manufacturers have a device called a weatherometer. This device is essentially a cabinet with racks for wood samples and lights giving off a specific wavelength, measured in nanoseconds. The weatherometer is an effective tool at comparing one product against another in identical conditions. However, these results do not gauge the product's ability to withstand the temperature variations, humidity, organic growth nor wood destroying organisms. The testing you want is actual exposure testing. There are test sites all over the country, but Miami, Florida's test site is the one that is the most severe. If you can get actual exposure test results on your product, then you can throw the brochures away. The bad news is that most stain manufacturers don't have the data, and if they do, they generally don't make it available.

Check with your local log home builders and dealers, and ask them about wood finishes. Ask them what they use, and how long they've been using it. Ask them if there is a place you can drive by that has had the product on for more than two years. Make an inspection up close. If you can't get any satisfaction, ask other log home owners. All wood finishes look good for the first few weeks or months, but you want to know what it looks like after 2 years or more. Research indicates that most natural finishes fail in terms of UV, mildew and water protection between 7 and 18 months. There are only a handful of finishes that beat the average. Your stain supplier should have a full knowledge of wood protection and be able to talk intelligently about the ones they sell, and how they compare with others in the marketplace.

A high quality finish is one that provides the best appearance and performance on your log home. It can improve the appearance and add value. An inferior product can save short term dollars and it may even look pretty good for several months, but long term maintenance could cost many times more than a properly selected finish in the beginning. Plus, *since the cost of labor to apply the product is often many times more than the price of the product being applied, it simply doesn't make much sense to waste money on a cheap finish.* The paint or stain usually only makes up about 25-33% of a painting contractor's price. The rest is labor, so choose your product based on research, reputation and price, not fancy brochures and smooth talking salespeople.

Chapter Seventeen
Sealant Systems

O ne of the biggest challenges a log home builder faces is preventing air and water infiltration. There are dozens of ways to notch a corner and dozens of ways to get an airtight seal between logs. Most of them are pretty good, but not all of them are 100% effective all of the time. When you take a living tree that stands vertical for 50-100 years, then cut it down and carve grooves and notches in it, stack it horizontal in a wall and smother it with oil, there's no telling what it's going to do. Manufacturers and log builders do a great job of making allowances for settling and shrinkage, but sometimes they get a rebellious log that just doesn't behave in a predictable fashion.

• *Notches and Corners*

The primary method of log home design begins with the style of house logs. Some notches are scribe fitted and designed to get tighter as the logs season. Some start with relatively dry logs and notch them tight to begin with. Some use elaborate single, double or triple tongue and groove systems with caulking and foam tape. Others use dovetail corners, saddle notches and the list goes on. It is difficult to say which one works best all of the time since there are many external forces at work, that the builder cannot always control.

Internal Seals

Usually there is an internal seal or an external seal, and sometimes both. Internal seals can only be seen in the cross section and are installed on the final job site. These seals include fiberglass insulation, foam gaskets, caulk, spines and the like. They are used when the logs fit tightly together and each log nests inside the one below. Examples are tongue and groove, Swedish cope and the log-in-log systems. The seal keeps out air and water infiltration by creating a flexible barrier that theoretically moves with the logs. There is a closed cell and open cell foam strips, and both can be very effective. Chances are that your log home company has done it's homework and selected the best one for the log system that they can provide.

External Seals

External seals are visible from the outside of the logs and can be installed anytime after the logs have been stacked. Examples include chinking, caulking, spray foam, moss, mud and mortar. Some log structures are designed to be chinked with a gap of an inch ore more between the logs. Others get chinked because of internal sealant system failure or for aesthetic appeal. Caulking and chinking are not necessarily interchangeable.

Caulking is much more elastic than chinking and is therefore much softer and rubbery feeling. Most caulks will probably get hard and brittle after several years, since most caulk is not built to withstand temperature extremes and ultraviolet light. Re-caulking is fast and easy as long as the finish does not inhibit adhesion. However, caulk is somewhat shiny and may not be the best choice to fill large voids. Also, caulk comes in a variety of wood tones and clear, so pick one that closely matches your wood color. Also, make sure it is rated for exterior use. Many caulks have warranties and theoretically, the longer the warranty, the better the caulk.

Chinking should not be used as an internal seal. It does not stretch as much as it needs to, and it has so much bulk it may interfere with other seals, like gaskets etc. Modern chinking is synthetic and stretches as the logs move. Modern chinking materials have a granular feel and look very much like mortar. It is not glossy like caulk, and looks more natural on a log wall. Chinking should be installed over a foam backer rod, which will be discussed later.

Log Movement

One of the biggest factors that all log builders have to contend with is log movement due to log settling and shrinking. Depending on the height of the walls and the moisture content of the logs, one can expect 1" to 6" of log movement in a vertical wall. Because wood is a natural material and sometimes has spiral grain, you may get twisting, shrinking and settling until it reaches an equilibrium moisture content with its surroundings. Movement may be reduced to a minimum, but still occurs somewhat. Log home builders make as many allowances for this log movement as possible, but it's impossible to predict how much movement will take place and where it will happen.

These big cedar logs with their bark intact, make an unusual doorway.

After several months the homeowner may feel a draft or see some water in the house after a driving rain. In a worse case scenario, you may see some daylight between the logs, or notice flying insects inside the house that probably did not come in through the door. Correcting these problems starts with finding them. If you notice that your heating bills are twice what they were last year, then you either have some log separation, or you may need to go close that window in the back bedroom. You need to find the leaks and seal them. Leaks should always be sealed from the exterior of the house.

• *Caulk*

Caulk works fine if the leak is restricted to a couple of small areas. High quality acrylic latex based caulks are generally pretty good to use, but don't skimp on the quality. You get what you pay for in caulk, so as a rule of thumb, the higher the price, the better the quality. Caulk can be purchased from log home product suppliers in a variety of wood tones, as well as clear. Don't forget about checks either. Checks are cracks in the logs that can cause water, air and insect infiltration. They should be treated with a borate based wood preservative first, then sealed with caulk. Regular caulk or a "liquid caulk" works great for filling checks.

• *Chinking*

In cases where the leaks are extensive, you may consider chinking the house. Modern chinking materials have evolved from the early days of lake bottom mud and cow dung, then to cement mortar, and now to high tech polymer based systems. Today's chinking materials are durable, elastomeric and should last for many decades. As far as the application goes, there are several basic guidelines you should follow. The first rule is to hire a professional chinking contractor to do it for you. Chinking is meticulous, monotonous work and requires working on ladders and reaching out past your center of gravity. If not installed properly, the chinking will crack and lose its seal. If you hire someone to do it for you, you can call them back to fix it. If you do it yourself, you are responsible for any problems that may arise. Having worked for a chinking supplier for several years, I can tell you that for the

94

most part, professionally installed chinking works perfectly most of the time. Homeowner installed chinking has problems most of the time. However, if your budget is tight and you have the time, here are some pointers to remember if you chink your own home.

The chinking bead should be at least 3/4" wide by 1/4" thick. You should always use either a backer rod or a bond breaker tape to prevent three point adhesion.

The band of chinking should be unbroken around the whole house. It should completely encircle

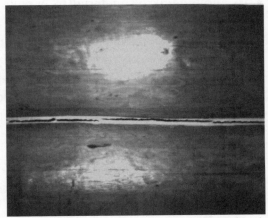

The chinking bead is too narrow and too thin. There was no backer rod. All of these mistakes resulted in a broken seal.

the windows and doors, not just go up to them and stop. It should follow the outside corner notches and continue all the way around the outside corner tails to get a complete seal. Interior chinking is not mandatory if the exterior is chinked. It is more cosmetic than functional. Chinking comes in a variety of colors to either contrast or closely match the log finish color.

To completely seal a house the chinking bead should be continuous around all windows, doors, laterals, outside corners, rafters, ridgepoles and corner tails. Also, large checks should be filled, especially the ones that start on the outside and go to the inside.

• A wider bead insures that the chinking will absorb the log movement. In other words, small diameter logs shrink less than the large diameter logs. By the same token, the chinking bead between two large diameter logs must be wide enough to stretch several times more than the chinking bead on a smaller log. However, if the logs are dry, and if the home is more than four years old, you can usually get by with a bead width as narrow as about 3/4", as long as the rest of the rules are followed.

• To allow chinking material to expand and contract with log movement, it must adhere only to the top and bottom of the joint. To prevent adhesion in the center of the joint, apply a bond breaker. Backer rods serve this purpose effectively. However, in the rare situation where backer rods are not installed, use masking tape, clear plastic packing tape, styrofoam, or any other material to which the chinking material will not adhere as tightly as it does to the wood.

• Chinking material should be applied and troweled to a finished thickness of at least 1/4" and up to a maximum of 1/2".

• A radiant heat source, such as a wood burning stove or fireplace dries the air and directly heats the logs and chinking. This can cure the chinking too fast and decreases its strength and elasticity. To allow the chinking material to cure properly, use the stove sparingly for the first 2-3 weeks.

• <u>The chinking material should always be applied no less than 3/4" wide and 1/4" thick. Backer rods should be used whenever possible.</u> This minimum geometry assures ample log movement when a narrow bead is desired. The exception is a log home that is over a few years old and most of the expected log movement has taken place.

• Blisters in the chinking material can usually be avoided by chinking in the shade. Either choose a cloudy day to chink on, or drop a tarp over the eaves to create your own shade if direct sun cannot be avoided. However, if blisters do form, wait a day or two, then take a sharp knife and puncture the bottom of each blister, then gently press it back down to the backer rod.

Chapter Eighteen
Checks and Grain Cracks

Checks are difficult to avoid in a log home. They happen as the wood is shrinking and are a result of stresses that build up within the log as the moisture is lost and the log is shrinking in diameter. Checks expose unprotected wood and can cause air, water or insect infiltration. All checks over 1/8" should be treated with a borate based preservative and checks over 1/4" wide should be filled with caulk or special check filling materials. The checks that require the most attention are those that are upward facing and on the lower logs, where they could collect rainwater deep into the log center, which could lead to rot. Also, when they begin in a

The ring shakes are splitting on the log ends, resulting in severe checking.

corner and continue into the house, checks may become a conduit for drafts, bugs and water infiltration. The third check to worry about is the one along a spiral grain. When the check is facing up and then spirals downward, water could eventually follow it into the house.

To deal with a check, first you treat it, then you seal it. A borate based preservative works great as a treatment for any rot or insect infestation that may be going on in the check.

All checks over 1/8" wide should be treated. However, it will be more difficult to treat the ones facing down since a liquid wood preservative will want to run right back out. In this case, you can make a paste of Timbor or Penetreat by mixing just enough water into a cup of powder to give you the consistency of cookie dough. You will notice the mixture will get warm, due to the exothermic reaction that takes place. Don't Worry! It's not going to hurt you. Take a small putty knife and shove this paste into the check making sure you get it in as deep as possible. It is not necessary to fill the check with the mixture as long as you get a good bit of it down or up to the depth of the check, although it won't hurt if you put a bunch in. After that, caulk that baby shut.

Reinspect your work after a few weeks and reseal any areas that need it. As these sealants cure, they shrink, and if you did not put it on thick enough, there could be areas that have ripped or pulled away from the sides. Therefore, make sure your sealant goes on at least 1/2" thick. <u>The log home needs to be inspected periodically for touch up and filling new checks.</u>

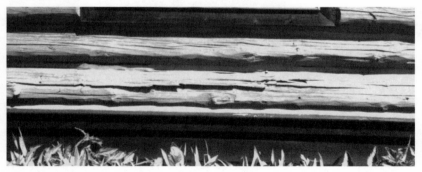

The upward facing checks trapped moisture and have rotted the logs.

Part Three

How to Clean, Preserve, Protect, Seal and Maintain Other Exterior Wood Structures

Chapter Nineteen
Decks

Decks are a great way to expand your indoor space to the outdoors. A well constructed and properly maintained deck can make a great place for entertaining, family dining and just relaxing and enjoying your little kingdom. Think about it, this is your property, you own the airspace above it and the many miles of dirt under it. Why not spend a few hours on a lazy Saturday afternoon thinking about just that.

After you're finished thinking, look down at the wood on your deck. What color is it? When was the last time you applied a water repellent? Is there anything to prevent UV radiation from the sun breaking down the lignin and slowly destroying the surface? Are there miles of checks and cracks? Any mold or mildew? Shall I stop here or shall we talk about the warped boards and nails that have to be pounded back into place very few months? OK, OK....I'll stop.

Don't feel bad. I'll bet 90% of the decks in this country look just as bad, or worse. In 1992, at the American Wood Preservers Association annual meeting, it was estimated that there are 6 billion square feet of deck in this country. If an average size deck is 500 square feet, that means that there are about 12 million decks in need of some degree of restoration.

Decks take a real beating from the elements because of the angle the sun hits it, the fact that it's usually damp on the under side and sun dried on the top side. Rain sits on it, airborne pollution and dust settle on it, outdoor furniture is dragged across it and people walk all over it. Ironically, most decks are built out of soft wood, like cedar or pine. The wood fibers get broken and compressed and pretty soon the deck that looked so good when you built it, looks like it has aged 100 years.

If the deck is pine, it has probably been pressure treated to protect it against rot and insects. However, the chemicals used in the pressure treating process tend to dry the natural oils out

Top: A close look at a deck in need of restoration. Bottom: Even from a distance you can still see what shape this deck is in.

of the wood, and boards check or crack and splinter. I've seen pressure treated pine decks that were less than 10 years old that needed to be replaced because they were so splintered and cracked. The wood will probably never rot and insects will probably never attack it, but because the *surface* did not receive proper care and periodic maintenance, it became an eyesore and it had to be replaced.

Cedar decks are more common in the west where cedar is abundant. However, there are many treated pine decks in the east that are being replaced with cedar. Cedar has the reputation of being impervious to rot or insects, and that's just not true. Old growth cedar, the kind of trees the spotted owls build their nest in, have very durable heartwood. These trees are 200 years old and their heartwood contains thujaplycin, which are what gives cedar it's durability. However, old growth cedar is just about impossible to get in the USA and what we do get, mostly comes from Canada. The cedar we get now is second or third generation hybrid cedar, genetically altered to grow fast. They are harvested at about 50 years and the heartwood is not only less abundant, but less durable than old growth cedar. Cedar is more dimensionally stable than pine and when properly installed, protected and maintained, it can last just as long as treated pine for decking.

The surface of CCA treated or cedar deck boards need to be protected from the elements to protect and maintain the aesthetics and smoothness of new wood. Because of the process that CCA treated wood goes through, it is best to wait at least 30 days after the deck has been built before you do anything to the surface. Cedar decks can be finished within a couple of weeks if the weather is fairly warm and pretty dry. There are many readily available products out there for decks. Make sure you prime the surface first, and use a high quality acrylic latex paint if it will be painted. If you are going to stain it with a transparent finish, use a high solids product. Low solids finishes just don't hold up more than a few months. Plan on cleaning your deck every year and apply another coat of finish as needed. The best products only last about three years on a deck and those are hard to find. Most over-the-counter products need to be applied once a year.

• *Cleaning the Deck*

If it is heavily soiled with lots of mold and mildew on it, plan on renting a pressure washer, or borrowing one from your neighbor. You know, the one that has every power tool in the world, neatly organized in an immaculate work shop, with hand tools outlined on the pegboard.... Go to a paint store, or a building materials store and get some wood cleaner. As we discussed in the chapter on wood cleaners, they fall into basically two categories;

bleaches and acids. Look at the labels under the precautions section for chemical names like sodium Hyplochlorite, calcium Hypochlorite or sodium Percarbonate.

These are best to use on moldy surfaces. Oxalic Acid-containing products are best on surfaces that are very gray. Read the directions despite your inclination to just jump right in and get started. Most of these products are concentrated and need to be diluted before use, so follow the directions. As a precaution, read and obey all safety instructions.

The best way to apply most of these cleaners is

Both views show a much more attractive deck after it has been cleaned and retreated.

with a garden sprayer. Make sure yours is not made out of something that the label on the cleaner warns against. Usually they are stainless steel, galvanized or plastic and are pretty well chemical resistant, but the seals may not be. Apply the material evenly, overlapping about 50% with every pass until the whole deck is covered. Watch your step, because it's probably pretty slippery. Allow the cleaning solution to "work" on the wood for about 15 minutes, unless the label says otherwise. Also, don't let it dry. If

104

it starts to dry in areas, mist it down with water. Scrub the surface with a push broom or truck washing brush. Make sure you get the corners and edges even if you have to use a hand brush. Do the rails at the same time, but be careful when working overhead with any kind of chemical. Eye protection is a must.

Another option if stripping, power washing or repriming doesn't sound like your kind of challenge, is to simply flip the boards over. The restoration will be much easier on wood that's never had anything applied to it. There is a special tool designed to pull nails easily, without tearing up the surface. I'm sure a reputable contractor-oriented tool supplier will have something besides a claw hammer he would love to sell to you.

• *Staining a Deck*

Start with the rail and balusters first. Lay a tarp or drop cloth on the deck to prevent spatter and drips from staining the deck before you're ready. Avoid application in direct sun.

If you have lattice, forget about brushing. Get a large piece of cardboard and attach it to the back side of the lattice, then spray it. After it's dry move the cardboard to the other side and spray the remaining side. Have a brush handy to catch any runs or drips.

To do a first class job, you need to stain the gaps between each board. Purchase a handful of small foam brushes to accomplish this task. This is a good job for teenage kids. It's what my father used to call a character builder.

After the gaps are stained, a paint roller and pad attached to an extension pole works great. Saturate the and roll out the first coat parallel with the boards. Lay it on pretty heavy. Then switch to the pad and apply a very light coat in the direction of the boards, making sure there is no puddling lap marks.

Chapter Twenty
Cedar Shake and Shingle Roofs

Cedar shake and shingle roofs are the largest use of exterior wood that are:

- *traditionally untreated before installation*
- *seldom treated with wood preservatives while in service*
- *totally exposed, receiving direct exposure to sunlight, rain, snow, hail and sleet*
- *neglected while it decomposes, then gets replaced with a less attractive, less renewable roofing material*

Cedar has been used as a roofing material for centuries. As a matter of fact, during the settlement of this country, wood shingle roofs were about all there were. Today, they are one of dozens of alternatives for the roof over your head, but despite the attempts of many, there is nothing out there that can beat the way a cedar shake or shingle roof looks. <u>However, the single most important reason to have a cedar shake roof is that through proper care and periodic maintenance, a cedar roof's useful life can be doubled or tripled.</u> This fact alone makes cedar shakes the most economical roofing material, with the look that only cedar can offer.

In a previous chapter, I said that wood species is an over rated concern for a log home, and that the way you take care of it is the real issue. However, when it comes to wood roofing, western red cedar is really the only wood species to use. Cedar used in shakes and shingles have a predominance of vertical grain, minimal knots, dimensional stability and low weight. However, the two most important reasons are it's natural ability to repel water and it's natural decay resistance characteristics. This is due to natural wood extractives, called thujaplicins. The heartwood of old growth trees has a much higher concentration of thujaplicins.

These natural wood preservatives make cedar a wonderful building material that will out-last most other wood in similar exposures. However, old growth cedar is getting harder and harder to find, and the cedar that is being harvested now comes from second or third growth forests. These trees are not old enough to have large quantities of heartwood with the natural decay resistance of their grandfathers. Therefore, their resistance to decay is not great to begin with and when installed on a roof they lose these natural preservatives quicker, through the intense drying effects of the sun and from rain washing them away and leaching them out.

The Life Cycle of a Cedar Shake or Shingle Roof

Once the tree is cut down, it's life support systems are diminished, and mother nature sends in the scavengers to return it to the earth. It's nature's way of recycling and it begins sooner than you think.

Our friend, the sun, is the first of wood's enemies to start the attack. The changes are part chemical and part physical, but overall it can be classified as weathering. The first change you can observe is a change in color from the initial brownish red to more of a silvery gray. This usually occurs in less than a year. At this point the damage is limited to the surface cells of the wood and is only about .01 inch deep.

The second line of attack is from mold and mildew. Mold and mildew spores are microscopic seeds of fungus. They are airborne, and everywhere! They grow whenever the temperature is above freezing and below about 100 degrees F. They do not destroy the wood necessarily, but they do increase its porosity, or its ability to absorb water. They also turn the wood a much darker shade of gray or black and often appear in colonies that look like ink spots.

Moss, mold and lichens on a wood roof. Left unmaintained, this roof will only last 10-20 years before it has to be replaced.

As the wood's porosity increases, it absorbs more water when it rains and takes longer to dry out. Meanwhile, two other things are going on. As the wood absorbs water, it swells. When it begins to dry out the wood shrinks. This continual process of swelling and shrinking during wet and dry cycles causes the wood to form checks or cracks in the surface. These checks and splits, trap water and expose new unprotected wood **_below_** the surface. At this point, the process of destruction accelerates to a much more severe level, since it is harder to detect and treat areas below the surface. The second thing that happens is tree debris such as pine needles, leaves and airborne particles settle on the roof and accumulate in the valleys or keyways between each shake.

This stuff also collects water and slows the drying process of the wood around it.

In the cool and damp Pacific Northwest, where cedar shakes and shingles are the most common roofing material, they can remain wet for months at a time. Lichens or moss begin to grow along the butt ends of the shakes, which spreads to the surface. This keeps the wood wet even longer. The mild climate, combined with a damp environment make an ideal habitat for decay fungi to step in and colonize. Decay fungi actually feed on the wood's nutrients causing a loss in strength and density. Decay fungi, also known as rot, will destroy a wood roof as well as any other wood used outdoors that is not properly treated with a good wood pre-servative.

This roof is in bad need of maintenance. Notice the moss growing on the ends of the cedar shakes.

Without any care or preservative treatment, this process can take anywhere from 10 to 30 years or longer before roof replacement becomes necessary. Much of this depends on what part of the country you are in, the orientation of the roof, the thickness of the shake, the roof pitch, the amount of sun and shade, and how much tree debris accumulates on it. However, as mentioned earlier, unlike any other roofing material, you can extend the life of a cedar roof by at least 50%, and maybe 300% or more.

Pretreating Shakes Prior to Installation

To get the **_maximum_** life out of a cedar roof, the shakes or shingles should be treated prior to installation. Since pressure treated shingles have limited distribution, you can treat them yourself by dipping them in a preservative solution for a couple of minutes, then allow them to drip dry before they are installed. This way the back side and edges are treated. After installing, this would not be possible.

The initial treatment will not last as long as subsequent treatments, because the new wood is not "open" enough to allow much penetration of the treatment. The good news is that it will not take as much preservative to do the job. The bad news is that you will probably have to treat the roof again in the second or third year. When you retreat the roof, there should be no organic growth to remove, and the only surface prep you will have to do is to sweep the roof and remove the debris from the keyways between each shingle. This treatment should last anywhere from 4 to 7 years before it needs to be done again. As before, surface preparation should be minimal although a light pressure washing may be necessary for this and subsequent treatments every 4 to 7 years thereafter. I sincerely believe that a cedar shake roof that is properly pre-treated from the beginning, and maintained every 5 years or so, can last 100 years or longer.

Cleaning the Roof

If the roof is more than a few months old, it should be pressure washed to remove organic growth and debris that has settled on the roof. Pressure washing is brutal on soft wood, like cedar, and should not be done any more than absolutely necessary. However, pressure washing a roof is the easiest and fastest way to clean it. Cleaners, bleaches and brighteners may be OK if you have a very small roof and don't have access to a pressure washer, but they are really not necessary when you have a good pressure washer. Pressure washing usually removes the upper layers of wood cells, which in most cases is where most of the grunge is anyway. The result will be a roof that looks almost brand new. However, a word of warning: At this point the roof is more vulnerable to decay than a new roof, since weathering has removed most of the natural wood preservatives that the cedar once had. It is critical to have the roof treated with a good wood preservative within a month or less, to restore it's ability to fight decay and organic growth.

Pressure washing is dirty and dangerous, and should be done by a professional that has the equipment and experience to clean the roof with minimal damage. However, it can be done by the homeowner if precautions against falling and wood damage are exercised. Pressure washing a roof is different than pressure washing a log home or a deck.

You don't need to be concerned with causing fuzzy wood, by excess pressure since you're not really after a furniture type appearance. On a cedar roof, you do want to remove the upper layer of wood and the associated grunge, whereas when doing a deck or a log home, you have to be careful to only remove the grunge.

Before you get started, it is a good idea to disconnect the downspouts from the gutters. You will be blowing off a lot of debris that could clog the downspouts, so it's best to just let if fall to the ground and rake it up in the aftermath.

Also, it is best to use a pressure washer equipped with a dual lance wand, so that you can reduce the pressure while you are on the roof. This enables you to rinse an area after cleaning and pre-wet it before cleaning, which will loosen some of debris, making it easier to remove.

It will be necessary to bear down and wash the roof hard to remove all of the stuff that's accumulated and is growing up there. Use a 15 degree tip, and don't worry if you have to hold it as close as 4 or 5 inches from the surface to get it clean. However, you should be able to get most of the roof clean by holding the tip 12 to 18 inches from the surface. There are areas that you need to be particularly cautious around because of the high risk of causing water leakage into the house. These areas include skylights, vents, ridge caps, chimneys and valleys. The best way is to hit them with a couple of quick passes and keep the spray on the wood only. You may even consider staying about a foot away and then come back and clean those areas with a scrub brush. Also, if you are equipped with a dual lance wand, you should reduce the pressure around these sensitive areas.

Tree debris is accumulating on the roof. Without maintenance, this roof will soon be destroyed. Pressure washing is the most efficient way to get all of the debris and organic growth off the roof, before treating it with a preservative.

Careless power washing can do more harm than good. There is a tendency for the inexperienced person to over-do it. The more careful and experienced you are, the more pressure and flow you can use. If you are inexperienced, keep your pressure under 2000 psi and your flow rate around 3 gallons per minute. The professionals usually use pressures around 3000 psi with flow rates of 4 to 6 gallons per minute.

Keep the wand moving quickly at all times. This is a very active sport and the movement is similar to sweeping the driveway with a kitchen broom, or raking leaves. Make three or four quick passes over the same area and move on.

A mossy wet roof is a very slippery roof. It is best to start at the ridge and wet down the section of roof you are about to treat. Then, from the top, clean the ridge and the first row or two of shakes all of the way across that roof section. Then from the ridge in the middle of that roof section, clean a 3 or 4 foot path all the way down, keeping your feet on the cleaned section, where you will have better traction. Then go back to the ridge, standing on the clean path, and reach over and quickly move the wand down the fall line about 3 rows, then go back up several times, as you clean another path about 3 feet wide down the roof.

When you get to the bottom of a path, turn around and clean the butt ends of each shake, as you work your way back up the clean path. Also, make sure the keyways between each shake is cleaned of debris that may have accumulated there. Once you finish a roof section, rinse it to remove any loosened debris that did not get washed off.

When the butt ends of the shake are punky from rot, use the pressure washer as a cutting tool and remove the rotten wood.

Don't worry about shingles which may be blown off the roof from the force of the pressure washer. They were probably rotten and were not serving any purpose if they were not properly attached. A new shingle should be put in its place when the other repairs are made.

Clean the surface of the shingles on your way down the roof, then clean the butt ends from the downhill side on your way back up. This gives you a much better angle to hit them at. However, you have to be particularly careful not to force water up under the shake and possibly into the house. The angle is critical here. Too steep, and you miss the bottom part of the butt end. Too shallow, and you spray water into the house. You must remove everything that is growing on the butt end of the shake. Otherwise, when you treat the roof, you will not get proper absorption of the preservative into the shake.

If the roof has extensive "old growth moss" you might consider using a moss killer first. This should be done when the moss is active. Give the product a couple of weeks to do the job. Potassium salts of fatty acids are a pretty good choice for this task. Look for it in the list of active ingredients of moss killers at your local hardware or building supply store. Once the moss is killed, it will be 100% easier to remove with the pressure washer, and if done correctly, will help to sterilize the roof. It will not prevent the moss from coming back, but the long term treatment should be even more effective if the roof is totally free of moss roots that pressure washing may not remove.

Safety

Use footwear that will provide good traction. Corkers are soles that you can strap onto your shoes, which have studs, like snow tires, on the bottom. They bite into the shakes and improve traction dramatically. However, if you step onto a shake that is not attached, it could become like a skateboard, so don't be over confident.

Use a ladder that meets all safety requirements. Be sure to set it on stable, level ground.

Place a 2 X 4 in the gutter to prevent it from bending under the weight of you and the ladder.

Make sure there is someone in or around the home to call if you get in trouble. Have someone check on you every so often, so if you fall and are unable to call for help, someone will find you before too long.

Plan your moves and don't get in a hurry. Never run on a roof.

Wear skin and eye protection when using any kind of chemical.

Have a properly rated fire extinguisher located nearby if you are working with flammable or combustible materials.

The ladder should extend three feet above the roof line for easier access to the roof. Tie it off at the top.

Use a rope or bucket to bring up your tools and equipment. Don't carry them up the ladder with you.

Whenever possible, walk across the roof, instead of up and down it.

Use safety lines and harnesses approved by OSHA for fall prevention.

Be particularly careful when working at the edge. In order to get the bottom few butt ends clean, you may have to reach out past your center of gravity. If you are not using a safety line, do this part from a ladder on the ground.

Replacing Shingles

You can make up to about 30 repairs or replacements per 100 square feet before you should consider replacing the roof. However, if the roof is more than about 20 years old, and has never been treated or maintained properly, you may consider reroofing the whole thing, since there is probably damage below the surface, that may be pretty advanced.

You will need tools for this: a roofing hammer (one with a hatchet-like blade on one side of the head) or a regular hammer and a mallet and chisel, a hacksaw blade or wire cutters, a wood block at least twelve inches long, a nail set, shingle nails (hot-dipped galvanized at least one inch longer than the ones already on the roof), and new shingles or shakes.

Use the blade of the roofing hammer (or the mallet and chisel) to split the damaged shingle. Split it so that the shingle comes free of the nails holding it down. Work the pieces out of the roof.

If the old shingle is of an irregular pattern that will be hard to match, try placing the pieces back together to form a template for cutting the new shingle. If this isn't possible, use a square and pencil to mark the excess as best you can and trim a new shingle to fit. It may take a few tries to get it just right; better to err on the side of taking off too little than too much.

Go in with the saw blade or wire cutters and cut the old nails flush with the underlaying shingle.

Drive a new shingle into the area left, by removing the old one. Only go in until the butt end is about one inch below the butt line of the adjacent shingles.

Toenail two nails through the shingle at a 45 degree angle; get as high up as you can without damaging the overlapping shingle.

Use the nail set to finish driving in the nails. This will help you avoid hammer damage to the surrounding shingles.

Place the wood block against the butt end of the new shingle and strike the block firmly with the hammer. Drive the shingle in until the butt is even with the butt line. That's it!

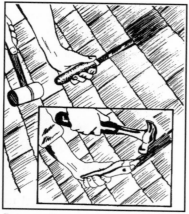

Remove damaged shingle by splitting it free of the nails.

Cut off the old nails flush with the underlaying.

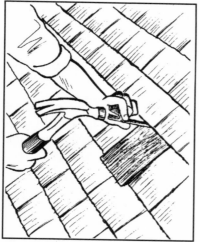

Toenail the new shingle at a 45 degree angle and set the nails with the punch.

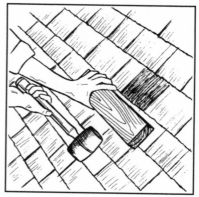

Place a wood block on the butt of the new shingle and tap it into place.

Undershimminng

If your shingle is split, but otherwise sound, undershimming is a good alternative to replacement, but if the shingle is rotted or loose, you will have to replace it. Undershimming involves lifting up the split shingle and slipping a piece of waterproof shim underneath it. This procedure goes quickly and is less expensive than replacing individual shingles. Because undershimming causes less chance of damage to a roof, it is recommended for repairs on older roofs.

The shims should be made out of heavy 45 bound roofing felt, aluminum or galvanized sheet metal, or thin shingles, even asphalt shingles.

Use a claw hammer to raise the butt end of the damaged shingle. Cut a shim larger than that of the repair area, but smaller than the shingle. Slip it under the shingle. There is no need to nail it down, as the friction between the wood and the shim is usually enough to keep it in place. Metal shims often have a rougher burr on the surface to keep the shim in place. The shim should be completely under the damaged shingle so that it won't be visible. Not only is this a neater installation, but the shim material won't weather the same as the cedar.

Lift the split, but sound shingle carefully with a claw hammer.

Slide the undershimming material under the shingle. Pre-cut it, so it's edges won't show.

119

Roof Treating Products

Since most people don't have the opportunity to dip treat their shingles or treat them in the first couple of months, let's look at how you can extend the life of your cedar roof and postpone replacement as long as possible. Even if the roof is 5 or 10 years old, you can double or triple it's <u>remaining</u> service life.

There are only a few choices of products for treatment of cedar shake roofs. Even though I have not mentioned specific products throughout this book, in this section I will. The reason being that these are specialty products and hard to find in certain parts of the country.

Unlike wood finishes for decks, log homes, outdoor furniture and fences, a roofing preservative has much greater demands placed on it. As I mentioned earlier, furniture grade appearance is not important.

There are products out there called shingle oils that may be OK if you live in a very dry climate and don't mind if the roof turns a silvery gray color. However, these products seldom contain any wood preservatives or UV inhibitors and are simply not recommended in areas where other cedar roofs have colonies of mold, mildew or moss on them. Nor are they recommended if the roof gets full sun exposure. An example of this product is Chevron Shake and Shingle Oil.

Water based products containing Copper Napthenate are good for control of moss, mold, mildew and some insects. The copper imparts a greenish cast which fades to brown after several weeks. Pigments can be added to the mix at the job to offset the green color. These roofs often have a distinct orange color. Despite their abilities to control organic growth and insects, these products do very little to slow down the rapid absorption and release of rain water, which results in checks and splits in the shakes.

Also, the pigments that are typically used are paint pigments and are more appropriate when added to a full colored paint. They do not have the color stability of a specialty pigment ground for use in a transparent stain. Examples of this product are: Shakelast by Atco Coatings and Cunapsol by ISK BioSciences.

Oil borne products containing Copper Napthenate are very good. They have stood up the best in tests conducted by Texas A & M's Forestry Department. They contain a high quality pigmentation system, an excellent UV package and utilize a nonoxidizing oil that penetrates deep into the wood with enough resin binder to toughen up the surface of old shakes. The problem with this product is that it can only be applied to roofs that are very dry when rain is not imminent for a couple of days. This product is called Radcon or TWP Shake and Shingle or TWP 200 Series.

Despite the limited market size for shake and shingle treatments, there will continue to be new products developed to protect cedar roofs against UV light, organic growth and water.

The methods in this chapter are proven

This 5 year old roof was pressure washed and retreated with TWP which added many years to it's remaining service life.

and have been used on thousands of cedar roofs for years and will be for the foreseeable future. If you have a cedar roof, you have to do everything you can to extend its life. It's not a one time deal though. Read on for ideas on how to get the most out of your cedar roof.

Maintaining the Roof

After the roof has been pressure washed and treated with a good wood preservative, about the only thing you have to do is keep the debris from building up. About once or twice a year it should be swept off or blown off with a leaf blower. The same level of fall prevention should be exercised when doing this, so refer to the safety section, or hire a professional to do it.

If you find a few shakes in your yard after a wind storm, and they are in pretty good shape, nail them back in their place using the procedures discussed. Make an annual inspection from the ground, using a pair of binoculars, to pinpoint any problem areas.

Wood preservatives that are applied after the roof is installed are not permanent. They will last anywhere from 2 to 7 years depending on the preservative, how it was applied, the geographic region and the orientation of the roof to the sun. When the roof starts to look faded, or dried out, it's time to consider retreatment. As long as you have it retreated before there is moss or other organic growth, the roof will not have to be pressure washed hard. It can be lightly pressure washed, which will minimize the damage and keep the wood intact. You may only have to sweep it off before retreating. Plan on keeping your roof clean and retreating it every 5 years or so and you will double or triple its remaining service life.

It is not inconceivable for a cedar roof that is cleaned and treated in the first or second year, then maintained and retreated every 5 years thereafter to last 40, 50, 60 years or more. Take care of the roof over your head. Cedar shakes and shingles are a wonderful choice of roofing materials. There is nothing else you can use that will last 2 or 3 time longer with proper care and periodic maintenance.

Chapter Twenty One
A Long Life for Your Home

Wood restoration is something that you should only have to do about once every 20-30 years if the home is properly maintained. I hope this book has helped you to understand the natural process of wood's life cycle. I also hope that you understand the chemicals and techniques you can use to protect and maintain the looks and integrity that makes wood so special.

When you are restoring a log home's exterior and you get down to bare wood, I strongly encourage you to use borate treatments to prevent decay and insects. I also encourage you to apply a good wood finish and maintain that finish whenever it begins to look faded, or no longer beads water. Whoever said that log homes were maintenance free was just trying to make a quick

sale. They are not maintenance free, they are maintenance intensive and worth every hour and dollar that you put into them. There may be a day when log homes will become a thing of the past...again. It may be because of wood shortages, government regulations or building codes. If so, today's log homes could become just as much a novelty and treasure, as rare as antique furniture.

Stay ahead of mother nature. Remember that once the trees were cut down, the defense mechanisms that helped them fight off disease and made them unappetizing to termites was terminated. It is nature's job to recycle itself, and between the fungus and the bugs, your house can become compost unless you jump in and take charge of the situation.

One last word on chemicals and safety. Whenever you are dealing with any chemical, protect your skin and eyes from accidental spills and splashes. Make sure that you read the precautionary statements on the containers and follow them. Wash good after a day of wood care and don't wear the same clothes until they have been washed. Also, be kind to our environment. Never pour any chemical down a sewer drain or anywhere that may lead to a water source. Dispose of empty containers in accordance with local regulations.

I have tried to be as objective as possible without mentioning specific products. However, I am in the business of selling products such as wood cleaners, brighteners, strippers, preservatives, paints and finishes. I keep an open mind and evaluate several new products every year. If you know of a product that has withstood the test of time, write me and let me know about it.

This is my first book and I'm sure there are typos, misspelled words and grammatical errors that got overlooked. Please accept my apologies and I'll do better in my next one. This is the first edition and I plan on updating it as technological advances make their way into the wood restoration and protection business. I would be most appreciative of any comments or feedback you may have, as well as suggestions for the second edition. There may also be a real problem with the wood in your home that this book does not address. Let me know and I will research it for the second edition and contact you with my findings.

Thank you for purchasing and reading this book. I hope that you are a smarter shopper for wood care products and have a broader understanding of what you're up against. Wood is a wonderful gift from our creator. Take care of it and it will take care of you.

Jim Renfroe

Part Four

Measurements for Product Estimating and Trouble Shooting Guides

Stain Calculations

Perimeter of House (L + L + W + W)=   _____

Wall Height=   _____

Gable Ends (L x H divided by 2)=   _____

Roof Overhangs (Width x Perimeter)=   _____

Deck (L x W)=   _____

Porch (L x W)=   _____

Porch Ceiling (L x W)=   _____

Total Square Feet of Exterior Wood=
(sum of all of the above)   _____

Coverage rate of the stain
you plan to use   1st Coat= _____ gals

                         2nd Coat= _____ gals

          Total Gallons Required=   _____

NOTE: Do not subtract area of windows
and doors. This is your contingency
so that you don't run out of stain in the
middle of your job.

TOP VIEW

Deck

Porch

FRONT VIEW

SIDE VIEW

Caulking or Chinking Calculations

Perimeter of House (L + L + W + W)=   _____

Log Courses=   _____

Lineal Feet of Logs=
(Perimeter x Courses)   _____

Contingency for Corners: _____ x 1.25

Total Lineal Feet=   _____

Multiply the lineal feet by 1.25
for corner contingency and use
this final figure for estimating
how much caulking or
chinking you will need.

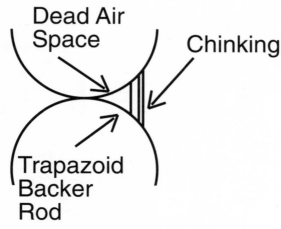

Dead Air
Space

Chinking

Trapazoid
Backer
Rod

NOTE: It is best to call your caulking or chinking supplier with this information and have them estimate your product needs.

Inspection Checklist

• *Outside the House and Above the Ground Level*

Problem	Solution
Windows and doors not properly sealed as indicated by drafts, wind noise or visible gaps.	Remove trim and seal the outside with caulk or chinking.
Flashing is absent or ineffective around doors and windows.	Install or replace flashing as required.
Flashing is absent or ineffective at roof/wall intersections.	Install or replace flashing as required.
Flashing is absent or ineffective at roof/chimney intersection.	Install or replace flashing as required.
Evidence of fungal attack on logs, steps, columns, deck or planters. Inspect by tapping with a hammer or probing with an ice pick.	Remove finish and clean wood. Drill holes and insert Impel Rods. Treat surfacd with borate preservative. Reseal with finish. Eliminate source of moisture.
Evidence of insect attack. Oval holes, termite tubes or tiny piles of sawdust.	Call pest exterminator or treat with borate based preservative if the attack is isolated to specific areas.

Problem	Solution
Logs that protrude beyond the roof overhang.	Clean and treat, or cut off so they are protected by the eve.
Water repellent finish no longer beads water.	Clean or strip as required. Reapply high quality wood finish.
Exterior finish cracking, peeling or flaking.	Strip and power wash. Inspect for decay and reapply a high quality wood finish.
Absence of any wood finish whatsoever.	Inspect for decay, clean and power wash, apply a high quality finish.
Fading or washed out appearance, especially on south and west walls.	Clean or strip as required. Reapply a high quality wood finish.
Color variation between top and bottom of same log.	Clean or strip as required. Reapply a high quality wood finish.
Presence of black mold or other significant darkening anywhere.	Remove finish and clean the wood. Treat with surface borate preservative. Reseal with a high quality wood finish. Eliminate source of moisture.
Checks larger than 1/8"	Treat with borate preservative and fill.

Problem	Solution
Cracks in chinking.	Repair by applying chinking to crack, then feathering out with a brush Or rechink that area with same color.
Check for chinking or caulking that is no longer adhering to the wood.	Remove and replace if it's caulking. Chink over old chinking with at least a 1/4" bead.
Inspect corners for logs that do not fit tightly together.	Caulk or chink all log corner intersections.
Inspect for hardened and brittle caulk.	Remove and recaulk or apply a bond breaker, tape and chink.
Roof overhangs too short and water is splashing into the logs, causing discoloration.	Install gutters, clean the discolored logs, apply liberal coats of water repellent preservative annually, or as required.
Gray, weathered appearance of bare wood.	Apply oxalic acid based wood cleaner, scrub then power wash. Sand if necessary.
Water stains on the logs, like where the sprinkler hits repeatedly.	Apply oxalic based wood cleaner, scrub then power wash. Sand if necessary.

Problem	Solution
Mushrooms or bracket fungi growing on the logs.	Replace those logs. For remaining logs above and below that area, use internal and external borate treatments. Apply liberal coats of water repellent preservative.
Soft or punky wood, when probed with an ice pick.	Use internal and external borate treatments, then apply liberal coats of water repellent preservative.
Sagging logs.	Probe for rot. If extensive, replace those logs. For remaining logs above and below the area, use internal and external borate treatments. Apply liberal coats of water repellent preservative.
Look for checks larger than 1/4" facing upward or spiraling near a corner that may collect water.	Treat with borate preservative and fill with caulk.
Check logs and ground for fresh sawdust.	Probably indicates an active beetle infestation. Call a pest exterminator or use borate based preservative over the bare wood.

Problem	Solution
Check for gaps at the butt joints of logs in the wall.	Treat with a borate preservative, then caulk.
Look for moss or mold on a wood roof. Also inspect for tree debris clogging the gutters and keyways between the shakes.	Pressure wash then treat with water or oil based preservative specially designed for wood roofs.
Mold or other organic growth on the deck or porch.	Use chlorinated wood cleaner, pressure wash, then apply penetrating oil preservative.
Check for firewood stacked against the house.	Move at least 50 feet away.
Check for standing water against the foundation wall or rain water flowing toward the house.	Bring in enough fill dirt to slope the ground away from the house.
Damp, moldy smell in the house.	Inspect crawl space for standing water. Also install plastic vapor barrier if one does not already exist.

• *Inside the House*

Problem	Solution
Check for a finish or protective coating on the logs.	Clean and apply a transparent film that can be easily cleaned. Product example would be one suitable for wood cabinets.
Mold/Mildew	Remove with a bleach based cleaning solution. Then apply a wood finish that contains a fungicide.
Inspect for signs of insect infestation.	Call pest exterminator or treat with borate based preservative if the attack is isolated to specific areas.
Can the walls be dusted easily?	Sand smooth and apply a transparent film that will not hold dust or grime.
Inspect all log intersections for daylight showing through.	Caulk or chink the outside in those areas that you identified.
Inspect for drafts on a cold, windy day or night. Carry around a container of water and keep your hands wet as you hold them close to the walls and corners. Drafts will be more evident.	Caulk or chink the outside in those areas that you identified. Consider sealing the entire exterior.

Problem	Solution
Inspect doors, windows, corners, roof/wall intersections and chimney/wall intersections for drafts, as before.	Caulk or chink the outside in those areas that you identified as leaks. Consider sealing the whole exterior.
Inspect checks for drafts, as before.	Treat with borate preservative and fill.
Check for air or water leaks after the home has been caulked or chinked.	Caulk the checks on the outside. Also, consider using a high resin clear finish to seal knot holes. Double check window and door seals.

Part Five

Sources for
Products
and
Information

Sources

This is a partial list of some of suppliers of the products listed in this book. Log Home Magazines are also a good source for materials.

Oxalic Acid Based Cleaners

Wood Care Systems   1-800-827-3480
    • Gray Away
The Flood Company   Available at most larger
    • Deckswood   building materials outlets,
Behr   home centers or retail
    • Deck Brightener   lumber yards.

Chlorinated Wood Cleaners

Wood Care Systems   1-800-827-3480

Also check at most larger building materials outlets, home centers or retail lumber yards. Look for sodium or calcium hypochlorite in the list of active ingredients.

Chinking

Sashco Sealants   1-800-767-5656
Perma-Chink Systems   1-800-548-3554
Weatherall Inc.   1-800-367-7068

Borate Treating Service

Orkin Pest Control   404-888-2742
    Dan Ledbetter

Wood Problem Consulting

Jeff Smith	360-341-7191
Chuck Stayton	903-834-3572
Bill Sittler	918-494-0543

Impel Rods

Wood Care Systems	1-800-827-3480
Perma-Chink Systems	1-800-548-3554
Sashco Sealants	1-800-767-5656

Bora-Care

Weatherall Co.	1-800-367-7068
Nisus Corp.	1-800-548-3554

Boracol

CSI	1-800-801-0078
Wood Care Systems	1-800-827-3480

Timbor

Sashco Sealants	1-800-767-5656

Penetreat

Sashco Sealants	1-800-767-5656

Pressure Washers/Accessories

Direct Line	1-800-241-2197
Northern Hydralics	1-800-533-5345

Strippers

Wood Care Systems	1-800-827-3480
Sascho Sealants	1-800-767-5656
Bio-Wash Corp.	1-800-858-5011

Caulk

Sashco Sealants	1-800-767-5656
Perma-Chink Systems	1-800-548-3554
Wood Care Systems	1-800-827-3480

Backer Rod

Timeless	1-800-524-3040

Wood Finishes

Wood Care Systems	1-800-827-3480

There are hundreds of suppliers of wood finishes. However, most of them will not last more than two years before fading and organic growth becomes apparaent. Armed with the knowledge that you have after reading this book, you will probably know more about how to evaluate a product than most service personnel at the local building materials outlet. You need a product with over 30% solids that provides water repellancy as well as protection from mold and UV light.